Sol Pineda

YOU ARE THIS INSTANT

A step-by-step guide on how to be more present through conscious action

Illustrated by
Marina Remmer

First published by Busybird Publishing 2022

Copyright © 2022 Sol Pineda

ISBN:
Paperback: 978-1-922691-85-9
Ebook: 978-1-922691-86-6

This work is copyright. Apart from any use permitted under the *Copyright Act 1968*, no part of this publication may be reproduced, stored in a retrieval system or transmitted in any form or by any means, electronic, mechanical, photocopying, recording or otherwise, without the prior written permission of Sol Pineda.

The information in this book is based on the author's experiences and opinions. The author and publisher disclaim responsibility for any adverse consequences, which may result from use of the information contained herein. Permission to use any external content has been sought by the author. Any breaches will be rectified in further editions of the book.

Cover Image: Marina Remmer

Cover design: Busybird Publishing

Layout and typesetting: Busybird Publishing

Illustrations: Marina Remmer

Busybird Publishing
2/118 Para Road
Montmorency, Victoria
Australia 3094
www.busybird.com.au

© Sol Pineda Wellness

Dedicated to every soul I've encountered.

To your soul, in the journey of getting to know yourself, moment by moment, through the eyes of love and presence.

To my dear mum Carol, my one-of-a-kind dad Alejandro, and my greatest teacher in this life, my brother Juan.

To my other half and partner, who has held my hand through making this happen, and my beautiful modern family.

To you, with all the love in the universe. And hoping we will cross paths again, soon.

INTRODUCTION

This book is intended to be a manual, a guide on the side, a set of tools or toolbox for YOU. You will find your unique way to go through it, this could be in the usual chronological order, or through following your intuition and selecting a page at random.

Its intention is to help you come back to the present moment, to each instant of your life, and decide HOW you want to live it, WHAT you want to see in it and WHO you want to BE.

This book is the result of many years and experiences I've had in the coaching and spiritual realm, and life itself. It is in honour of all those teachers, masters and guides who have been a constant inspiration to live and create a different life.

Thank you, to you all. And to you, the reader and next manifesto of a life that will inspire others to think outside the box, to connect with love and presence, and become the person you are intended and supposed to be.

You can do it. And I'm honoured to be by your side.

With gratitude and love,

Sol Pineda

CONTENTS

CHAPTER 1
YOU ARE THIS INSTANT 1

CHAPTER 2
THE CHANGE: ANICCA 7

CHAPTER 3
LIVE LIFE IN EACH MOMENT 19

CHAPTER 4
TAKE RESPONSIBILITY 25

CHAPTER 5
LET GO AND ACCEPT THE DANCE 34

CHAPTER 6
SET INTENTIONS 46

CHAPTER 7
CREATE YOUR FIRST AID TOOLKIT 62

CHAPTER 8
BUILD A ROUTINE 96

CHAPTER 9
CHOOSE THE NARRATOR OF YOUR STORY 111

CHAPTER 10
RELEASE JUDGEMENT 129

CHAPTER 11
CELEBRATE MAGICAL MOMENTS 150

CHAPTER 12
BACK HOME, BACK TO LOVE 153

ABOUT THE AUTHOR 165

ABOUT THE ILLUSTRATOR 167

Chapter 1

YOU ARE THIS INSTANT

There is a part of your being that is reading this page right now, reading the words that have been flowing through my pen. This part of your being understands the concept of this instant and what it is all about.

I believe a part of your consciousness is living moment to moment, with full awareness and presence, through every step of your life. We may forget this sometimes and you may find yourself caught up in a story that tells you otherwise. It could be a romantic and beautiful story, or a drama-based one with fear and uncertainty. However the story looks it doesn't really matter, the fact is it might have the capacity to take you out of this present moment, from this instant. And this my friend and soul adventurous traveller, is what we are going to experience and return to again and again during our journey together throughout this book.

A couple of years ago, in my twenties, I recognised my capacity to 'leave and escape' from being in the present moment. I remembered a truth I had long forgotten.

I am not the drama and violence of the world around me. I am not the beliefs of unworthiness and limitations that have built up in my mind like a secret spy doing its job while I'm 'asleep'. I am this instant. This consciousness that lives in this moment, this part of a whole that has everything and maybe nothing, with all possibilities of creation and change.

If I truly am this instant, I can create my life moment to moment – how I want it to be, how I want to feel, and how I want to perceive the world. Right?

This is what I'd like to share with you through these pages, so that you too can remember. You are always creating your life, and you can make this journey as peaceful, calm, loving and full of presence as you want. We will start with the self, with exploring your true self. There will be an introduction of many examples and situations of my own experience as a way to reflect how close and similar our paths may be.

As I said before, it had been 27 turns around the sun or so (and maybe a lot of past ones too), before I had this moment of realisation. It was a huge process of questioning absolutely everything that I had learnt, considered myself to be, and where all the stories around my beliefs started.

'YOU ARE THIS INSTANT.' It was written in graffiti around the corner from my grandmother's house in Buenos Aires. I often used to visit her in between business meetings, rushing from one side to the other of a city of 14 million other souls running around and 'trying to survive' another day.

I had seen this sign more than once, and more than twice had decided to ignore it. I probably judged it for its reckless colours and painting. It was definitely not the most beautiful graffiti I had seen, and yet something inside me, a part of my being would connect with it every time I passed through the same street. It was something beyond the mind, something that I will call consciousness, your being, the truth or simply love.

I would have a couple of 'mates' (Argentinean drink) with my abuela, and talk about life and romances (oh yes, my failed romantic life was a full chapter of our talks, you could say). I would smell her flowers, walk through her garden barefoot as we remembered ancestors and where each species of flower comes from, and she would collect some dead leaves and flowers and trim others. Sooner rather than later my phone would ring with something important, and I would have to go, or 'leave' the present moment.

'I wish you would stay longer,' she would always say.

'Me too, but I have no time.'

That was a phrase I lived by in my survival mode life. 'I have no time' is another way to say I am not the creator of my reality or this instant. 'I have no time' says I am being forced, manipulated, or pushed into other people's agendas even though it is not who I truly want to be.

Quite challenging, right? Who likes to admit that we are going against our own will, against what our being and highest consciousness wants? And yet, this uncomfortable truth was one of the first realisations of what I call remembering my truth. Yes, I am this instant.

Others could say this was a glimpse of an awakening, when you understand or see yourself as whole, as the I AM, as the creator – instead of the victim of everyone's stories.

Seconds after feeling complete presence and admiration for the now, my mind started questioning absolutely everything. And when I say everything, I mean exhaustingly questioning it all.

What am I doing? Do I love what I'm doing now? Would I rather do something else? Why am I doing this then? Why am I living in the city if all I want is nature and to live by the sea? Am I a failure in all my relationships? Have I done anything that I truly wanted? What do I want then? How do I create a life where I live in this moment, connected to this instant every time?

A world of infinite possibilities had opened, but a whole parallel story of fears, doubts and negativity started battling this new realisation. The fact was, something needed to change and whether I was ready or not, it was already happening.

Have you had a moment of profound realisation of the self? From there, you know this is it. Something is different, something has changed, and it might be something even greater than yourself, or what you knew about yourself till then.

It's like someone giving you an open ticket to the most wonderful place you've ever dreamt of going, with no due date – it's up to you when you choose to actually get on the plane and start the flight. And there's no turning back, because you've got your ticket and this is where you truly want to go. A seed has been planted – so germination will begin.

I like to call this germination a process of change. You can call it impermanence, evolution, or whatever comes to your experience. Please make this your guide, so re-write any word if something else resounds with your soul. I won't get offended. On the contrary, you can scribble on this book and make notes, write on it, highlight parts that you want to come back to. Set your pace and follow your heart – some of us take millions of moments, of instants to go through a full book. Others will take half the time or less. There's no rush – nowhere else to go, nothing to do, just being here and now. Listen to your heart and soul, it is whispering your truth. It is inviting you to open up and let change happen.

Chapter 2

THE CHANGE: ANICCA

Annica in Theravada Buddhism is the belief that all things, including the self, are impermanent and constantly changing. It is the first of the three basic characteristics of existence.

If we are this instant, then it means we are constantly changing, evolving, transcending, and creating. Change is a constant and life becomes an experience of impermanence. To view things in this way, or start perceiving every instant as it is, will mean a lot of change will come to your awareness and life. You will start to realise the sudden change in your thoughts, in your mind, in your speech and communication, in your feelings and emotions – and basically in all the world around you.

Your environment – the earth, the stars and space, the air and the water – everything is in constant change. Now, you will become aware of it.

As a kid I used to have brief moments of the awareness of this change, during the seasons, for example. Autumn would take me to a more contemplative state, looking at the leaves changing colours and falling, while admiring the cycle of life and death over and over again. Often my dad told me that even as a baby I would have this look where I narrowed my eyes, turning my child expressions into an adult trying to understand or remember something. I can see now how many of these glimpses or moments came from a higher consciousness than what I could understand.

Those feelings and sensations of complete presence and oneness, as I was surrounded by trees and falling leaves, awakened me to a whole new world, to that instant of feeling and being one with nature.

Change (and especially a big change in our life), sometimes brings resistance, or a feeling of aversion. As I said previously, there's a part of yourself that needs no explanation and really understands change, because it's happening right now. Every cell of your body, organ, your skin, every part of you being your whole environment, even your thoughts if you let them go wild, are experiencing a never-ending cycle of change. However, many of us, when we have to make a 'conscious' decision or jump into that leap of faith towards 180-degree change, tell, think and repeat to ourselves that change is not possible.

We say this is who we are and change is not possible. 'I've been like this all my life, this is who I am.' Our jobs, career and CV can portray who we are and our personalities too, even our family history. Plus, we might live a life we don't completely love or feel inspired by. We feel 'this is it', that there is no time to think about change. 'I can't.'

Famous last words.

For the sake of being 100% honest in this journey we've started together, I am writing this because a part of me has been there for quite a while. Please don't judge yourself for anything but try to foster that Zen 'beginner's mind'. Address any or all resistance and repeated behaviours that are not letting you live your life at its fullest, so that you can bring all the parts of yourself to the light and shine your fullest potential.

If you want to add an extra kick to it, we can bring in humour and make it a lighter recognition. Oh yes, so many times I've repeated those same words – 'I CAN'T.' Was it true, however? Was this ever your truth?

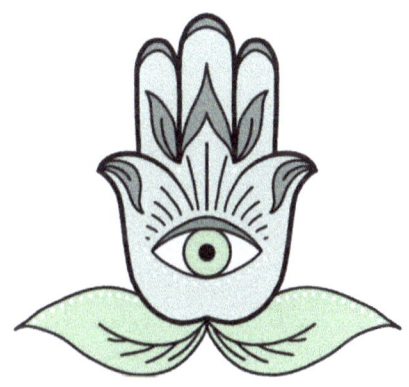

EXERCISE:

I invite you to write a list of the things you think you are or that may not change. On the left side you can write your limiting beliefs or resisting beliefs, on the right side you can go beyond resistance into what you truly are and want to be.

I left some blank spaces below for you to write in this book. Remember, this is up to you – if you prefer to use a separate worksheet, that is ok too.

RESISTANCE OR AVERSION	BEYOND RESISTANCE AND INTO LOVE
I am a failure	I am a constant creator and I live the life that I desire
I am trapped in this body that is not the one I like	My body is my temple and I can choose to re-create every cell in it every single day
I am not enough because …	I am grateful for being here – today, for this breath and this instant and I am pure love on earth

One of my main challenges when it came to change and resistance, had to do with one of the pillars that constitute our sense of self; my relationship with myself and my body.

I had lived for years not being able to even admit to myself that I felt a prisoner of my own body, its shape, its curves, how it looked and changed constantly, feeling out of balance at times. The list of things that I thought could not change when it came to this topic was immense. Many days, nights and moments I felt this was never going to change.

Have you said this to yourself before? Like a self-boycott where you are suppressing and eliminating all other possibilities by conditioning and telling yourself over and over again that this is never going to end.

As many others have said, and you probably heard before, this is NOT IT. You can now regain the confidence in yourself and choose love again. The book *A Course in Miracles* has a very powerful quote (if not all of it) where it explains that actually, you are not the victim of the reality you have created or come to believe, and in any case this can always change, and it depends mainly on you.

That IS IT, and I am going to repeat this for you: you are not the victim of your life, you can change any cause or area that may not be working for you anymore. Once you do, then you can surrender to the magic that will reveal moment to moment as you decide to live your wildest dreams. You can create the life you want, surrounded and in love with life again.

Change for me started in my twenties. It struck me in the heart after a series of 'rock bottom' events. I was living this rushing city life, kind of on repeat mode. When we live on repeat, it is like a part of you is dormant, but you have a sense you are about to wake up. The consequences of life beyond that point may be so different to what you are used to, that you may be scared to even listen to its whispering and murmuring ... It's like a part within you knows that there is something out there, that you could be living your highest potential and changing the world, helping others, living inspired and smiling and in love with life, but ... but ... but ...

THE WORDS YOU CHOOSE TO TALK TO YOURSELF MATTER.

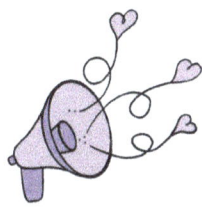

I did this amazing course once where we learnt with a dear friend, coach and psychologist about the importance of conversations. And this of course includes those going on in your mind. When you think about something and then you add the word 'but', it is like cancelling all that comes before that. It's like stating, 'I would like to live the life of my dreams, but ...' That's it, you are telling yourself, the universe, your mind and spirit and everything around you, that after all those dreams, you don't really think that you are good enough to pursue them or worthy of living them. Instead, why not trying to use the word 'and'. Give it a try while you observe how the conversations change.

I want to live the life of my dreams AND I am going to commit at this moment to create it and start the process NOW.

Change is already happening, so if you resist, the only thing that will persist is what is not serving you anymore. Maybe an old story or conversation going on inside your mind of who you once were, may be limiting you to actually own this instant.

People talk about finding their lives.

In reality, your life is not something you find (but), something you create.'

- David Phillips

You are a constant creator of your life.

To understand this or remember it all the time – it took me, my soul and body to let go of absolutely everything in order to give change some real space.

My belief around my body made me suffer, and so I acted consequently. I would deplete it from food, or binge eat – not finding balance or a healthy routine for every moment that life presented.

I moved alone after finishing school, so making decisions like skipping meals, or emotional eating (from guilt, frustration, fear and anxiety) kept me for a while stuck on the idea that I couldn't change my eating habits in this lifetime.

After a big heartbreak, one of those 'hit rock bottom till the very bottom' (what many call the 'dark night of the soul'), these patterns, fear, and disconnection with my true self and sense of trust became crystal clear.

There was a profound feeling inside me that this could not keep on going this way – and by 'this' I mean mainly my beliefs, thoughts, and fears around the future and past. I had already dedicated enough energy and attention to these fear-based stories that keep me stuck in feelings of unworthiness and pain. The fear of the future always looked like the worst-case scenario, with loneliness and unhappiness making everything dark and obscure. It had ruled the show for long enough.

Leaving the moment has many ways to express itself. It can be through thoughts and stories in your mind, going over the same narrative about the past, repeating the pain and the darkness that you've felt, and trying to avoid it all through habits like drinking, partying and drugs. I had tried it all. And all those choices just took me to the same place, a part of me being in total and absolute discomfort every single day.

When you are going through this rollercoaster in life, there might be times where you can appreciate the present moment, such as a full moon coming out in front of the bay, or a sunset surrounded by friends. And then, that inner voice that is so used to working in a certain way starts to become louder, telling you, 'Oh yeah ... this is happening BUT you are not this ... plus you've probably forgotten that you don't have a partner anymore and you look absolutely wrecked ...' Pressing 'play' in that rollercoaster of discomfort, drama, and unworthiness that starts again through the loss of connection with your true self is quite easy to do.

There's nothing 'wrong' with these stages. If you're going through the dark night of the soul or have been there before, you know that it may look like all it is all tears, lack of energy and love, feeling hopeless and hurt, getting to the deepest part that for so long you had been trying to avoid - and yet, a small part of your being, maybe just 1% knows that you are there to question it all, to start again, to regain trust in yourself and your life and start living in a new conscious way. It's from being through the darkness that we can acknowledge it and bring it back to the light - becoming responsible for who we really are and what it is that we are here to do.

How do you want to live your life? In repeat mode or in a constant adventure? Saying 'I can't'? Or, finding and building up the strength and commitment within to make it happen?

RISE ABOVE YOUR OLD CONDITIONING TO FEEL YOUR TRUE POWER.

When change knocks at the door and the dark night of the soul has shown you that rock bottom has only one way out and it is going up ... THIS is the moment to rise above your old conditioning and start re-creating your new life, moment to moment. Choosing love instead of fear, trust instead of doubt, kindness instead of hatred and guilt, and compassion instead of judgement.

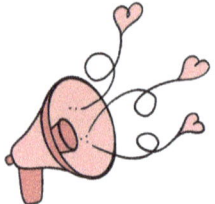

And where does it all start? Well, my friend, the answer is one you probably know. Where everything starts, all the stories, voices, ideas and beliefs that you may have created – within yourself, in this instant. Inside of you. Here and now.

Chapter 3

LIVE LIFE IN EACH MOMENT

This is a guide on how to live moment to moment. There are some steps that will surely help you along the way, and I will share them with you as you become the creator of your life, the narrator of your story, the awareness of what is happening in the now. We will focus mainly on you, starting with your persona and then moving to the whole.

Living life in each moment, being present with what is happening around or inside you is all about awareness. About being aware of the voice in your head, the thoughts you might be having, the stories developing, what is happening around and what others or your own true self is trying to tell you.

Life can be lived in each moment, by practising presence. This means coming back to the present moment or bringing your awareness to the moment you are in right now.

I realise how this is sometimes easier said than done. However, my promise to you is that if you practise, if you show up to tell yourself and remind yourself of the now, if you follow guidance and certain tools or simply commit yourself to be here and now, it is possible to start living in a whole new way.

For some, this happens after an 'AHA' moment, hitting rock bottom and coming up, or an enlightening experience. For others, it is about repetition and the number of times you come back to remind yourself that you are here and now.

It may also be a combination. You may have already experienced that enlightening moment and now you realise you can, and you want to return to being present. Life is constantly changing. This moment will pass and it's all we have. So my challenge or invitation to you today, is to make the best of it and try to be fully present day by day, in every instant. Then you can bring the best of you to the surface, to the light, for others to be enlightened by your gift and to pass it on to those who may need your inspiration.

The moment you start becoming aware of each moment, you will find that even without wanting to, those around you will feel inspired. They will want to share and know more about how you do it, what they can do, and how you can help them. And as this is something so natural and true for all of us, underneath all those layers and projections that we have created, it will easily flow and keep the wheel of inspiration turning.

What does it mean to live an inspired life? Simple, that you are fulfilling one of your major purposes here on earth, being of service and giving to others - offering what you have to give, offering the light and parts of your being that have come out of the shadow and can now help others.

Have you ever had a moment where you felt connected to inspiration and thus inspired a friend, your daughter or son, or a neighbour? Maybe it was just being creative, and letting that creative force come from the source of yourself and express itself. It might have been through a dish in your kitchen, through some words or a quote that you shared. When you choose to live life inspired and inspiring others, then you accept the responsibility that you do have something to offer. You do have something that is unique within you, and one if not many souls are waiting to hear from you. You understand that it's not only for artists or musicians to inspire and live in inspiration - it is for us all.

Being inspired happens in one miraculous moment. It only takes one instant, one breath, one 'AHA' moment - and you go 'BOOM, this is it! I now will share it with the world.'

However, many of us, who can feel constantly inspired, tend to surrender to that voice that says, 'But, hold on a minute - who am I to inspire others? Who am I to believe I can be an inspiration?' And there you go, just with that one thought, you come out of the present moment and into doubt and judgement. And guess what? There is no inspiration there. That force and power that you feel when you are connected to the belief that you can achieve your wildest dreams - it can vanish in just one instant.

So, for when this happens – or if you have caught yourself falling into this trap – that's all good. We have all the forgiveness and power within us to let that go and start again. And when you start again, in this instant, in this moment – you can truly believe that you are here to make a change. That the world and those around you, are waiting to be inspired by you – to be touched by this magic wand of all you have to offer. It may not be the same as what you had to offer years ago. We are talking here about the now, about what you can bring into this present moment to make your life more filled with magic and love.

When was the last time you felt inspired? What were you doing? What were you listening to? How did it smell? What were you wearing? Can you remember? Can you go into that moment and feel what it felt to be in the flow of inspiration?

When was the last time someone inspired you? Who was that person and what were they doing or saying?

I want you to go back to these moments to show you something – there was probably not much going on, or you didn't have to make a big effort. This force and light of inspiration, creativeness and presence does not need protocols or procedures, it's about simply being. And where does it all happen? You know the answer by now, my dear friend. It's here. When you are here, you are effortlessly doing what you came to do. You are fulfilling part of your mission and purpose. You are being of service to others and to the world with your presence.

Let's see now how we combine this consciousness and presence with our human side – aka the working mother, daughter, son, husband, wife, or taxpayer. Because yes, both can live together and complement each other. They can act as reminders and partners in the same scene. We can be spiritual beings in a human experience and human beings in a spiritual experience – and both sides can learn from the other.

Spirituality and different life experiences brought me to this understanding, feeling and embodiment of consciousness and presence. I then chose to become a health and wellness coach – study for it, practise, and really immerse myself into it. And what was one of the best things this choice brought me? I had the awareness, and that was great. I could realise when I was leaving the moment, when the words that I was choosing and saying did not resonate deeply with my being or were out of alignment. I could become more and more aware of my thoughts and actions ... and, what to do now?

This is where the coaching stepped in - now, let's create some action. Let's keep on moving. There have been great lessons from stillness and silence. Awareness has made me more complete, more present, more alive - so how could I combine it all and create something new, instead of falling into old patterns? Two words: conscious action.

Chapter 4

TAKE RESPONSIBILITY

Whether you like it or not you have always been the captain of this ship. Some courses and storms may have been on cruise control or repeat mode, and your usual answer may have been finding guilt or the responsible one outside yourself - aka your parents, your childhood, your job, friends, school, etc. Truth is, no one can make you anything if you don't allow that energy to happen. Things don't happen because of the outside, because they just are and you are the victim of all circumstances - they are created within.

Sometimes you may have found it was easier to blame certain feelings on somebody (the outside) or go back to making your parents responsible for what was going on in your life.

As much as your parents and childhood, or other people's comments can have an impact on your story, the one that has been repeating those thoughts and having these habits is you. It's always been you.

Whether a decision was made from your genuine self or from a set of conditions and limitations, once you realise how you want to live and feel now, then it entirely depends on you, and you can move forward with conscious action.

You can choose how to respond to everything and anything that shows up in your experience. If the way of life, job, career, relationship in which you wake up every morning does not serve you anymore - why not explore something different now?

Why not allow change to take its course, instead of staying in repeat mode, like if your life was a movie with a director that is not you.

Exercise:

- ◊ **What are your wildest dreams?**

- ◊ **What have you envisioned your life to be like? How do you envision your best possible self?**

- ◊ **Where would you like to go next and radiate your love as you unravel your true genuine self?**

What if all of this happens?

What if I make it?

What if you make it?

Maybe just like me years ago, you have all of this vision, and your vision board is full with pictures of women radiating health, fitness and peace – Buddha and nature, a house in the bush, being by the ocean ... and as much as you love looking at it, a part of you thinks, 'Yes, this is great, but ...'

I was there, had all the vision, all of the attempts and opportunities. And yet there I was, always listening to that small voice saying I am actually not quite sure change is possible ...

Please write below how it will look like if you make it all happen. You can also draw or make it a visual exercise.

A sense of chill over my body, maybe even fear arises when I ask myself 'What if?' Like when you think, 'What if I win lotto?' and next instant you are thinking about all the ideas of why you won't win it, dismissing that idea or dream, suggesting to yourself that you are not worthy of it or don't deserve it.

In order to allow change to happen you might have to start by observing yourself - becoming responsible for what your thoughts and stories are and sitting down with the darker parts that make up your whole as well.

After saying this, I want to let you know that having the ability to respond to something does not necessarily mean responding as in doing. As I've grown to understand, this response may be being able to observe - simply look at yourself, your thoughts, emotions, what is rising up and what story you are repeating - and breathe.

Breathing is the best way to stay tuned with the present moment - to be here and now. Meditation, yoga, walking and running all have one thing in common - conscious breathing, attention and focus on the air coming in and the air going out of your body.

Whenever you are experiencing strong emotions or something rising in yourself, you will notice that your breathing will automatically change. As you observe this you may want to become the captain of your breath as well. Just breathe in consciously and deeply as you exhale longer breaths.

As I became responsible for my journey, and more responsible for feelings arising within me, my capacity to respond evolved with this. During my teenage years I recall being a young girl trying to prove her point. I proved myself out of a story of not being listened to, respected or considered. Whether that came from a particular childhood event or a perception and story that I had created in my mind, I realised after a couple of years that this response was not being true to who I am.

I didn't know how to voice it and many times during the day I could see the story inside of me developing and deepening the trauma of not being accepted, good enough and the fear of being rejected. I went through the day wishing I could forgive whatever had happened or was going on inside, and just tell myself that the other voice inside my head was not truly who I am.

As I learnt later, most of us have a common fear to be who we truly are, our genuine self. Almost a collective thought-based idea that if we are the loving, compassionate, kind beings we are here to be, we will be condemned as weak, airy fairy or not good enough. So, like many, I developed this over responsible and defensive personality, but it was never who I really was.

A competitive environment and belief may be restricting you now from being who you truly are. When this happens as kids, and we just roll with it instead of questioning, we can develop a self-image and opinion of ourselves that is not really who we are and learn to operate from there. You may be realising that a part of your survival mode took you to act, be and relate in a way that is not necessarily your truth. You may also want to experience and be open to change NOW.

Most of us were raised like this, not because our parents intended to make us less lovable or kind, but because it was how they had learnt. It was what the collective society agreed on. You have to build a personality that can bear living in this hard world. And this includes not being perceived as 'too soft or kind', avoiding bullying and mistreatment and trying to reach to the top, regardless of what's happening to you physically or emotionally.

During these days, between competitiveness and being defensive and trying to reconcile with who I really was, I realised that all I wanted to BE in this world was a kinder person. That was my true drive - kindness and compassion. I was studying economics in university, and everything was about profits, income, expectations and diagrams. What was developing within me and what I was truly learning about humans and our behaviors, was a whole other degree.

I started to see more and more of the light, the love, and its opposite too – fear. The parts of me that I was not happy about, the stories that were not coming from a place of love became crystal clear. Without realising, my constant questioning of the world and how we choose to perceive was opening the door for the next decade of my life. A deep exploration and self-observation of the world around and beyond me. I gently started to repeat that I could choose again how to see life and my perception of every moment. I could start all over again. Every day, every moment.

Yes, I loved my parents and my childhood and all it came with. Yes, I had grown to be a successful student with A grades. Yes, I had some friends, not as many as I felt I would have if only ... If only I would let myself just be me. With no 'shoulds' or costumes or masks.

And so it began. Responding differently meant many times to not do as expected. To feel lost and 'not knowing'. To choose to start again and maybe even observe the same thing. Reminding myself that I AM the only one that can create or change my reality.

It meant becoming responsible for all those dreams and aspirations that had to do with a world filled with brothers and sisters, and love and nature. It meant that I could no longer blame others for what I had not yet achieved – because after all, it was and had always been my life, my responsibility. It meant finally, it was time to take the reins of my life and make it happen.

'Make it happen' says the neon sign on my beautiful stepdaughter's bedroom. And she surely does.

This is what she is choosing. It is her responsibility to make it happen ... and she is only ten. So that means that we can all do it, wherever you are now – you can start to become responsible for everything that you have left aside and still want to create. For all the inspiration that you must give and receive. For all the dreams and kindness and love that you want to explore and expand.

Let's keep moving, shall we? Because the journey has just begun. Conscious action is a series of interlaced chains that create a path. It doesn't matter when or where you start – the only thing that matters is that you begin.

Chapter 5

LET GO AND ACCEPT THE DANCE

However this looks for you, you've got to make space for the new.

I remember a dear friend, one of my soul mates, once calling me to ask me how I let go. She had a show coming up on the radio station she was working at and the topic was letting go. I had come to her heart as a voice that could express what this meant in a way.

What does it mean to let go? The opposite of grabbing, I guess. Grabbing or feeling attached to something probably comes from the fear of not having. An idea of scarcity, of lack, that this moment or instant (or thing) will not be here in the next moment. That this feeling I am having now will not persist. That this too, shall change.

As human beings we are surrounded by change, and yet so many times we find it difficult to embrace it, to understand it as something constant that is happening all the time. Thus, as a response to this misunderstanding, we create feelings of attachment.

We get attached to things, to brands, to cars, to a particular job, a person or relationships, to a place, a country, a society. We even get attached to problems, sometimes we get attached to problems big time. We also feel attachment towards the past ... or towards a story of a future that has not yet happened.

We may feel attached to nostalgia and expectations. When we feel so attached to everything that we cannot even enjoy all the wonders of what we have now, we start to 'think' about letting go. I say 'think' because this is how my process started. During a long period of my life I would repeat to myself, 'Let go, let go of everything, just let go.' I would ask myself, 'Why do you feel so attached?' And of course the process was coming or happening from a thinking mind. Why? What for? And I would let go of something, and then get attached to the next thing.

I let go of my clothes, for example. Heaps of beautiful designer clothes, and soon enough started to buy again, to fill up that void, that something that I was scared of not having. I would let go of a job, and soon start asking myself what am I going to do now with my life ... and before even giving myself time to be, I would be on the hunt for a new job.

I also had a time where I would let go of relationships, and although that felt harder, within the next couple of months I would develop a new one to hold on to with all my heart. So yes, I was letting go in a way, only I was letting go and grabbing the next thing over and over again.

And then one day, when my soul started to see and walk other ways, so did I. In that particular moment there was nothing to get attached to and nothing to let go of. I had an instant of awakening to the truth that I needed to truly let go – and learn to walk through life again. And so I did that day, walking through rice fields with no destination or plan. Without knowing if I was going to sleep in a warm place or find shelter that night. I just felt like I was taking my first steps in life all over again. I didn't have a job or a future so to say, I didn't have a place at that point that I felt I could return to. Mostly, my sense of self, my personality, my whole story of who I was just dissipated into thin air in that instant, on that one step.

For a second, I remember feeling so deeply empty. That everything in my body indicated I was about to start crying and go into an emotional breakdown. However, the body knew what to do and I kept on trusting the mechanics of each step, each walk. And all of my senses started to feel different. My smell, my voice, my touch, what I was seeing in front of me.

That day, I started a journey towards the unknown. I didn't know where I was going, I didn't even know what I wanted. Everything that I had known and clung to was not there anymore. Out of the calling of my soul there was nothing to be attached to! What was I going to grab?

The answer was nothing. I slowly started to feel less attached to life, mine and everyone's – as hard as it may seem, even my loved ones. I realised that desperately wanting for everyone to be alive was also a thought. It was a fear I had been clinging to because of the uncertainty of what not having them physically meant.

To let go of the fear of death was one of the main steps of this journey. Death is everywhere, right? Happening all the time ... However it's also a big taboo in many cultures, or it is associated with an ending. And that can get both scary and into the attachment side of things as well.

I lived a very safe childhood, and my parents always gave us shelter and protection. When I started growing up, getting out of that loving home bubble, things started to change. I started to see more; more of what I've never seen before. Walking through the streets of India was one of those sudden realisations and awakening moments to a truth I had been ignoring or not wanting to see for a long time. Death is actually everywhere, it is around us all the time.

At that point, I realised death had always been by my side. It was only the feeling of a young body and what I've chosen to see so far that didn't let me recognise that truth as something else in life. As just another moment, that sooner or later will come.

Letting go of the fear of death is probably one of the biggest, if not THE fear to let go of. It doesn't mean you're suddenly open to death happening. But in a sense, the part of your being that had been trying to cling to life is released, vanished, and a feeling of ease and peace arises.

You could say when you get to that moment, that a part of the self dies. And that is what happened in my case. I lived that realisation in that moment as the death of me. And the moment after that, everything in my life looked absolutely different – changed forever.

For the first time, instead of repeating 'I got to let go,' I started doing something different. This was the moment I started to accept, to truly accept that everything is constantly changing, being born and dying, repeatedly. Just like the lawn at your house or your neighbour's, grass going from one green to another, like flowers that come up in spring and in autumn trees losing their leaves. We, as human beings, are constantly changing from one season to another, one moment to the next. The whole universe works in this way – everything is in constant change.

When we can let go and accept that everything is changing – then we can let go of the fear of uncertainty, the fear of death, to this moment finishing right now. Because it is happening, it is changing and finishing and a new moment is starting and so you can accept it NOW, and truly let go.

Once you allow this to sink in, you no longer need to make an effort to let go. You become a human being and you start to BE, instead of constantly doing. When we are, we simply accept and there's nothing else to do.

The universe has infinite possibilities. Each day, we can create our life, our reality, this moment – totally different from what it looked like yesterday, with all the changes we want to introduce.

You can now live in a new place, a new house, a completely different country. You can create a new job, a new relationship, a new friendship or soul meeting, experience, a landscape, feelings ... everything!

When you accept you have such a power – so immense that you can create in each instant as you want – instead of thinking you have to let go, you become in tune with the natural cycle of constant change. Everything, like the Buddha said, including feelings and emotions, has the same capacity of arising and passing away.

This will free space in your mind and soul to start creating the absolute new instant that you want now.

Ok Sol, it sounds easy when I read it now. But how do I actually practise letting go?

Shall we try this short exercise together and see what comes out of it?

Exercise: Practise Letting Go

Breathe in deep and exhale. Repeat 4 times.

Connect with your true self, and ask yourself: what are the things or beliefs that have been holding me back?

Can you be honest with yourself?

I know that the fear of not having the right words or skills to write has been holding me back from writing this book. By becoming honest and putting it out there, I started to accept and sit down with my beliefs. Soon I was ready to let them go. Suddenly and magically, on a sunset afternoon with my family, I told myself this is it. I accept all past beliefs and fear of not being good enough, of failure or rejection and I am NOW ready to be who I want to be.

Please use the following space to write down the beliefs that have been holding you back, release old stories through your pen and let them go:

Now that you've written this declaration of honesty, call a friend, a family member or your coach. Go past the fear of being stuck here. Recognise the fear, own it, take it out of your system and declare that you are vulnerable to open your heart to it and ready to allow healing and light to enter this wound.

During the next 21 days keep on coming back and observing these fears, stories, or thoughts as they arise. Because they will. The ego will want to become loud and make sure you hear the scream, from all past beliefs and stories, to keep this on repeat mode. You now know it's up to you to create, decide, choose and become responsible for all these stories, and make something different happen.

Breathe in deeply.

Exhale.

Be ready to let go.

Spiritual note: I have learnt that the ego can be like a chameleon, letting us think that we have let go even when we are just creating new attachments to stories and concepts. Sometimes the fear of letting go too much may also make you doubt what you are doing.

When we start the practice on how to let go - like everything - we can make it a daily practice as well. At the beginning maybe it feels easier to let go of material stuff or whatever is filling you up with clutter. You may then move on to thoughts, stories or bonds that you are ready to let go of and make space for the new.

For those in a deep spiritual practice and path of remembering who we are, and that we are just One, letting go can go a step deeper.

After the realisation that all this is just an instant, you may feel that all future and past can be completely let go for good, a feeling of emptiness may arise within your whole life. You may start asking yourself if we are just an instant, this spec moving and changing already as we speak, why have plans? Why have intentions, dreams, or desires?

This may feel wonderful at the beginning, and the chameleon of our ego may adapt to this new environment and create other colours and shapes for its survival. This experience of recognising, remembering or enlightenment can feel different to each one of us. And how we move forward is different too. Some of us create a certain feeling of superiority once we recognise a truth. Others may feel empty or find that nothing has much meaning anymore. The ego's illusion and power may take you on a rollercoaster of all the above.

As I read these words, a part of myself, probably a new shape of my ego, wishes I had read this before. When I was feeling that sense of superiority and illusion that I had let go of everything, or when I turned to see life and all humanity as hopeless and meaningless, ready to leave this body and earth. Or even when I shifted and got stuck in a profound feeling of emptiness with the wholeness that life is – feeling there was nothing really to do, a purpose to follow, or content or truth in anything.

I can now understand these moments where my ego was shifting, only to create a 'new' or 'better' self where I could feel a slight sense of belonging and comfort.

What I'm trying to underline here is that even when we practise letting go, our sense of ego will still be there – shifting and maybe becoming more subtle. We can refine and practise observing it. Observing this sense of I – the ego self – that wants to capture every moment. Just hear that voice when it comes, without feeling a need to attach to it.

Every day as you practise letting go and observing, it will take you to the next experience. There is less suffering and less attachment, and you will feel at least, for that moment, that you are living completely in this instant with peace and ease.

'When you give more attention to the doing than to the future result that you want to achieve through it, you break the old ego conditioning. Your doing then becomes not only a great deal more effective but infinitely more fulfilling and joyful.'

- **Eckhart Tolle / Stillness Speaks**

Chapter 6

SET INTENTIONS

When you set your intention you are creating a direction towards your desires.

We all have desires. Even when we think we may have detached or let go from them, there is still a desire to survive, to have a peaceful and joyful life, to thrive at whatever we do or are, and to serve, help or inspire others.

Sometimes in a world so over-stimulated with all the media and messages going on, we can become 'lost' or out of balance with our true desires. When this happens, one of the most powerful things to do is to truly, completely listen to yourself now.

What is it that you really, ultimately desire now? Desires are ultimately the most intimate space and voice that we have within. That one voice that truly knows beyond conditioning and what others want from you - what you truly want for yourself in this life, in this moment.

Note: I find it important to note that desires can and will probably change. What you desired a year or decade ago may not be aligned with who you are now, or where you are now. And that is ok. That's why it's so important to keep on checking in with yourself and that inner voice. Keep that intimate bond expanding as you go through life. Observing and becoming the observer will bring you a lot of insights, and with those you can choose what to do, who to become, and who to be in each moment.

You may have had a lovely childhood for example, and your parents, happily married, wished for you the same experience - to get married and experience a life with someone by your side. However, your true desires and the calling of your soul may be different. Not less loving, or incomplete, just different. I've chosen the example of marriage, and this also applies to having kids, to your career, to your lifestyle or where and how you want to live. The ones around you, family and friends, may wish or want for you to experience something similar to them - out of love, generosity, hope or the need to control. Wherever this comes from it doesn't really matter. The most important voice for you to listen to and trust, is the voice that speaks from your heart.

Take a moment to reflect on the following questions:

- ◊ **What is it that you want?**

- ◊ **How do you want your life to be?**

- ◊ **Are you willing to observe and explore your true self and allow change to happen?**

- ◊ **Do you feel you deserve everything that you wish for?**

I love introducing to my clients the Deservability Act from Louise Hay's workbook, *Love Yourself, Heal Your Life*. In this act you repeat and say out loud that you know what you deserve beyond all conditioning and other people's beliefs. That you honour everything your parents/caregivers have done, as you've grown to be the person that you are now and open your heart in this moment to everything that you truly deserve.

I suggest you have the following quote handy and that you read it every day:

Everything that I desire, I deserve.

I deserve to be happy and to live my wildest dreams.

You deserve to explore the world, if that is what you wish for. To become radiant and inspirational, healthy and wealthy, if that is what your soul calls for. To be of service to the world and a catalyst for change. You deserve to shine your light and your love. To succeed in what you love. To see life through the eyes of love and fall in love with it every day. You deserve love – all the love in the world. You deserve it all.

Once you realise you DO deserve everything, you become responsible for manifesting every moment as you want it to be. And the next step, showing up for yourself, mastering your attention and perception of who you really are.

You may have many ideas and concerns regarding who you are and who you will be. You may have goals you want to achieve, yet feel so distant that everything you create in your thoughts is more distant. However, once you start recognising the responsibility that you have, you start to live like all these dreams were already here. Like they are already happening, and this is your truth and who you are. You shift your creative attention to what you want to manifest now. This is the main difference between wishing for something to happen and making it happen. Where your attention and your mind go, energy flows.

When you let your attention get diverted or affected by external causes, words or things that may happen, you start to distance yourself from the now, and from your full potential at creating this moment.

If you want to feel radiantly healthy, absolutely wealthy, magnificently happy, start feeling that. Embody it now, like if it was already here – because in another dimension it is already happening.

Focusing on who you are, instead of who you are not, changes the whole deal. When you focus on who you are, it's like calling the divine within you to be present here. And the only thing you will feel is complete. Grateful, blissed in love and joy.

There are some wonderful meditations and 'I AM' affirmations that I recommend you start exploring. Meanwhile, I would like us to develop together who you are, and remind yourself daily of your desires, everything that you deserve and already are.

I AM – Please complete	I will share my I AM's with you as an inspiration
	I am enough
	I am love and I am loved
	I am a source of inspiration
	I am an absolute creator of every moment

Sometimes you may need to start with the things that you already know, such as 'I am a successful writer and health coach.' Although this could sound superficial or an understatement, if a tiny particle of your being needs to remember you are ALL – the effortless creator, the well-known actress, a wonderful loving mum, a peaceful joyful being – this will help you to build that confidence and focus. Ultimately, you may have the realisation that you are ALL, that you've always been everything – that you are God too.

The incredibly challenging part of desires is that we have to feel them and trust them – deeply as if they where already happening.

You may have had moments in your life where this felt impossible. Working on an hourly rate job and just being able to pay for your weekly bills, for example, can be a contradiction to the feeling of abundance in the present moment. Nevertheless, if you can, practise and become the observer and look at the bigger picture. You might have been incredibly strong and healthy at that point, or had moments of silence and deep observation. Maybe you had more time with friends and family. What I am suggesting here is that sometimes, that voice that plays victim and goes on repeat mode in your head, is not necessarily what is happening in your reality. This may be difficult to accept or to let go of.

When the I AM feels absolutely present in this moment, create space to visualise that I AM with all its details. Let's say your I AM is abundant and attracts prosperity into your daily life. This is one of the I AM's that seems to be the most challenging belief to accept and focus on for many people.

Become that full, prosperous being in your vision. How do you look? What are you wearing? Where are you? Who are you with? Most importantly, how are you feeling and being?

Can you deeply connect with that feeling? Can you feel in every part of your body, in every cell, what it is like to be your prosperous, abundant self?

Write in the next few lines, in precise details, how this I AM feels, how this I AM is.

....

....

....

....

....

....

....

....

....

Take a deep breath, and keep this visualisation in a sacred space. Breathe in. Breathe out.

Your next step, is to trust. Let's surrender this vision as if it's already happening, as you are now. This I AM.

Now think about your road map. All the I AM's in your life, your desires, and your ultimate wildest dream life. Create a vision, see yourself in every step, in every way – moment to moment.

Use the following quick guide to setting intentions. Remember to begin with your ATTENTION – so pay close attention to what you are doing.

A QUICK GUIDE TO SETTING INTENTIONS:

1. **Start by listening to your heart. What do you truly want?**

2. **Don't listen to the voice that tells you it is not possible and gives you a list of excuses of why not. Challenge it with 'What if …?'**

3. **Bring all the positive and detailed feelings that you feel accomplishing this intention.**

4. **Feel it as if it was already here.**

5. **Believe that this is beneficial for you and all those around you. This intention is for the highest good for all.**

6. **Be ready for the universe to respond to your wishes and intentions. Stay open and allow creative action to happen.**

7. **Know that different paths may take you there. Keep a flexible and adaptable mind.**

8. **Trust that there is a higher power, God, spirit, ALL, that will help you achieve what you want.**

The quality of your thoughts and presence in this moment will create what you have intended. If you have been stuck in a negative pattern and keep experiencing similar or the same things, you may want to review how consciously present you are, here and now. Are you going back to trauma or past experiences? Are you repeating a past moment that has nothing to do with your present moment? If so, review previous steps to let go and start again. Always set your intentions from a clear space, both in mind and body.

How we use our attention depends mostly on our state of consciousness – fear or love. Desires that originate from love that come from your true self, will become fulfilled. If your desires come from fear, agitation or doubt, they will be harder to fulfil.

This has been my experience, and the experience of many women who strongly and deeply desire to heal their relationship with their body.

For many years, my desire was to have a body that I loved. The word 'perfect' for me, kept me coming to my knees and praying night after night. It was definitely one of my most repeated prayers. I remember being a teenager asking God to please help me have the body that I wanted, a fit and good-looking body where I could be comfortable and happy. What I was not conscious about at that time is that this wish, this desire, came from a troubled and confused mind. I was not coming from a place of love, wanting to be healthy and balanced. It was rather coming from a place of confusion, trauma, comparison, hate and attachment to limiting beliefs.

I remember clearly that night after crying in my bed alone. I had tons of thoughts and stories of despite, hatred and discomfort. Sobbing, I asked to be free. I asked God and my angels, everything in what I trusted, 'I just want to be free, be free in this body, free from all these stories and thoughts.'

That day, I believed in something higher and I surrendered my desires. As time went on, addressing the fact that what I was lacking was not another cardio routine, diet or regime, but self-love and more love, I started to desire and visualise myself and my wishes from a place of pure love – knowing that this was the key to setting myself free.

Both my feelings and prayers changed completely – and so did my daily reality, my wishes and ultimately my body. The miracles and wish of being free is my reality today. It took me a whole decade to understand 1) What I really wanted, 2) What to ask for from a pure consciousness and state of love, and 3) The how, to surrender to something higher and let the achievements come in their own time.

I look at the beginning of my story, where I was during those days with so many clients. And the one thing that I bring up before any detox or nutritional roadmap, is self-love. I can also see the resistance and attachment to the story of hate and fear. 'Yes, I know that I have to be kinder, but I am such a idiot, I don't know why I keep on doing this.' As much as part of them is desiring to change, there's a strong voice wanting them to be stuck, telling them it is impossible and ignoring the call of self-love.

If this is happening to you in any area of your life – with your body, the foods you eat, your exercising routine or the pressure you are putting on yourself and your career – it's time to pray for freedom and bring the love back to you, baby! The more love you put on the table, the smaller the voice that tells you 'You can't' and 'You won't' will be. The lighter you will feel and the happier your every day will be.

As one of the most famous functional doctors, Dr Will Cole says, and I repeated to myself for so long – you cannot heal a body that you hate. You cannot heal a body that you don't love.

Two days ago, I was giving a yoga class and a client brought up the topic of discipline. This concept had been going around in my mind for quite a while. Yes, discipline is a place to start or aim for at the beginning of your journey. In order for your mind to understand something new, we may need repetition. Discipline also helps when we want to establish a routine. Being constant in your desires, wishes and speaking them out loud, journaling, showing up for your daily self-work, creating your vision and meditating on it ...

Nevertheless, I'm happy to tell you that there comes a point – and you might be around the corner – when all these steps get integrated into your daily life and thoughts. You start to act and be from this place of love, abundance and magnetism. When this happens, you become free. You are free to choose and act from fulfilment and love. There is no need to keep on repeating every step every day as a tough routine. (Although don't get me wrong, depending on your personal reality and your personality, it might help.)

You begin to listen with more attention and become clear with what you truly want. You know for sure now that love, positive thoughts and feelings are the landscape in which you are painting your work of art. You finally let the universe do its thing, knowing you are safe and are being guided towards love again.

Pay attention. Trust. And love. Add more love, and more love and finally surrender. And once you surrender, surrender even more.

As mentioned previously, many of you have experienced the limiting belief that you are not abundant enough. Even having everything and more from Source (with capital S), I can understand and see this kind of limitation in others and what it feels like, as I've been there before.

Having an abundant mindset, being a wealthy person, attracting wealth and creating money – it all comes from your thoughts. What you repeat to yourself is what you become.

Having said this, it is easy to fall into the desperate feeling of 'not having' or 'not being' enough. Even millionaires go through these stages and they may feel that bills, wages to pay, mortgages, debts, insurances and investments that take them to a place of not feeling enough.

I'd like to return to one of my favourite teachers, Dr Wayne Dyer, on the matter of who you are. He explains that when you keep wishing for something to be in the future, 'I will be wealthy once I ...' or 'I wish I would win lotto one day,' on a subconscious level you are telling yourself what you are not now, in this instant. Therefore you are repeating over and over again in the following instant, what you don't have.

The moment you connect with the divine and everything that you are, now, here, 'I AM ALL,' and you start making it part of your thoughts, beliefs and imagination, you start creating what will be here in the next moment. In other words, you have to program yourself to believe that you are already what you want to be – I am a perfect body, I am wealthy and a magnet for miracles, I am pure love and peace, I am kindness – in order to make it happen in your experiences.

Let's say you have a troubled relationship with money and the source where it comes from, such as your job or career, or the system in which you live. Most likely, this feeling of separation from love will create an obstacle in the flow of energy and attract another type of attention – the opposite of what you have been longing for.

Many of us, in the search of something different than the usual capitalism or systems where we live on, have been called spiritual blah, hippies or airy fairy because we don't agree or flow with the whole. Having majored in economics, I have studied each type of system quite well, and for many years I understood the so-called supply and demand and how everything apparently works this way – although a part of me felt a strong rejection and judgement towards it all. With time, I got to see further than the ideals or political views, into a space where I always go back to when in doubt – a self-reflection and deep questioning if this doubt, thought or action comes from a place of fear or a place of love.

A deep truth and realisation for me, was that my judgement towards how things work around money was not connecting or coming from a place of love, but rather one of judgement, resentment, and even guilt.

After a lot of courses, journaling and going deep into this 'issue' or limiting belief, I came upon a course by Marie Forleo, owner of B-School. She suggested using the mantra 'I love money' and playing with it. I must be honest with you, my first reaction was one of judgement. I had to refer to this mantra for quite a while, without necessarily owning it. Although there was resistance, I could see what was missing in my equation regarding my finances and magnetism for money. It was simply and clearly one thing: love.

Louise Hay also uses a mantra, where every time you pay for a bill, service or invoice you come back to gratitude and tell yourself, 'There is always more from where this comes from.' You are grateful or thankful for being able to pay for the service and what you receive from it. Can you feel how already thinking like this connects you to wholeness rather than scarcity?

This is something you can start applying from this moment onwards. Next time you pay a bill, instead of coming from a place of guilt, scarcity or lack, just know that the universe is abundant and there is always more from where this comes from. When you are honoured to be able to use the service or pay for a certain thing, you honour yourself and the business or provider.

Again, it's one instant. It's one shift from saying, 'Oh no, the power bill again, and it's even higher ...' to 'Thank you Universe. I appreciate the electricity and the power that I have to run my home and keep everything warm and ongoing. I pay it with respect and love. And so it is. I accept more abundance from the source of where this comes from.'

If the universe feels like too much or you want to thank the company/business or God, please go ahead – make all of these mantras your own. They don't have to sound like the ones I'm suggesting. The more you find your truth, the more you will come up with your own inspiration and inspire others. What a lovely, complete and supportive journey for us all!

Chapter 7

CREATE YOUR FIRST AID TOOLKIT

Now we will explore together what works for YOU. What does your first aid kit for returning to this instant looks like to you?

One of the most powerful tools to return to this moment is nature. I can't stress enough the importance of a connection to nature, for you to live present and in this moment. For we are nature. We are natural beings connected with all and nature. We depend on nature. In nature we find food, nutrients, vitamins, hydration, oxygen and the truth of the inner connection that exists between us and everything – all of us.

From a scientific point of view, being connected and immersed in nature can help to lower blood pressure, regulate stress hormone levels, reduce nervous system arousal and strengthen the immune system function. It can increase self-esteem and reduce self-doubt, reduce anxiety and improve your mood. Violence, self-abuse and aggression lessen in natural environments, which also helps speed up the rate of healing of individuals going through this.

Psychiatric studies have found that being in nature reduces feelings of isolation and anxiety and helps with depression and mood swings. From a spiritual and holistic perspective, nature brings us to the present moment. Swimming in the ocean, smelling a flower in the garden, planting a new herb or walking in the park or by the river. It all brings us a sense of being, of belonging to something else rather than just ourselves, belonging to all.

When you start to observe, you recognise that nature is a constant reflection and manifestation of impermanence. Everything is constantly changing, moment to moment in nature. And so are you, so am I, all of us.

The seasons changing, leaves falling, days becoming shorter, the snow that melts from the sun, rivers flowing, sea levels rising and falling with tides and the phases of the moon – it all reminds us that nothing is stagnant. Things are happening NOW, in this moment. And as the Buddha said, 'This moment too shall pass.'

Nature works in an aligned and magnificent way. It is powered by strength and love and connection, as we human beings are – seeking for that one thing, to be connected and a part of it all.

We do this in our work, by selling things in a shop, a service or sharing our creative work – art, writing, movies. What we ultimately are always doing is connecting. Many times, however, we fall in this ego judgement of not being connected. We fall into the trap and limiting belief of separation. Whenever we vibrate from a space of fear and doubt, confusion and hatred, we ultimately are separating ourselves from the source of all love and acceptance.

Going back to nature is one of the easiest and most straightforward ways to come back to connection. If you ever feel lonely and separate from love, try going out into nature, for at least two hours wherever you are. Feel the holy presence of everything that is dependent and connected in the natural environment. Take deep long breaths as you observe.

Sitting down in nature, and walking, are some of the main practices that have absolutely changed my health. If there is something that we could all do with more experience and practise more of, it is stillness and peace. On this beautiful planet earth, we have developed such a fast pace. Running from one thing to the next, from one instant to another, trying to capture things on our phones. Plus, all the information and stimulus around us can make it very hard to unwind and stop, observe and be still.

> *It is in nature and stillness, where we can connect with our true nature of BEING rather than DOING.*

> *It is in stillness where we can learn to deeply listen to our heart, soul and even our mind.*

> *It is from stillness that we create.*
> *And it is with stillness that we heal.*

Nature brings the effortless opportunity to become still. When you are immersed in nature, think about those sunsets or sunrises. Think about the moon coming up through the mountains or behind the trees, illuminating the water with its golden light. It is in these moments, in those instants (where a part of you may be urging to take a picture or immortalise that moment), that another part of you is in complete presence and in awe of the wonderful experience.

That deep breath, that feeling of content that nature brings, comes together with stillness. Stillness may sound challenging for you today. Maybe you have more than one job to attend to, a family and kids to take care of, your phone constantly demanding your attention. No matter what your life is like today, at one point, one day, one instant, you probably felt this stillness, and with it your full presence in that situation.

Can you recall a moment like this? If so, know that this is something you can go back to. You can keep on experiencing and practising and bringing this kind of awareness into your life again and again.

Some of us like to plan for retreats or have moments during the day where we can be present and still. Meditation, a solo time, sitting down in your balcony or garden, a moment in a park. If you are starting to realise this wonderful part of your BEING and how much this instant means to your whole coherence and life – then I would suggest you start making time for yourself to be in nature (even more) during this week.

You may want to go for early cold-water dips in the lake or ocean like some of my clients do, or have walks around the park, gardens or coastline. You may plan for some gardening dates with yourself or just remain barefoot in the grass or soil. Whenever and whatever you plan on doing, aim to make it a priority at least for three hours a week, and see how you feel about it.

Studies have shown different evidence when it comes to our contact with nature. The truth is we are increasingly becoming more of an indoor species, sedentary (in front of a desk or device), sitting down and spending most of our time in offices, cars and enclosed spaces. This way of acting keeps us apart from nature instead of increasingly a part of nature. This may be a way that we 'evolved' or developed, as nowadays we don't have the need to hunt and gather and move according to the weather or seek shelter. However, we do thrive and become our optimal natural selves just by going back to those primal, caveman practices. It happens with movement and activity, it happens with food and with the sun, the moon and the stars. There are certain things that we are meant to keep on practising as natural beings.

Many of us have forgotten how to forage or hunt for our own food, how to produce it and take care of our soils. We have forgotten even how to breathe deeply with awareness, and to be in contact with the earth beneath our feet. All this, nevertheless, are instinctual qualities that we have within – we just need to remember.

Whenever I'm coaching and I have a client who lives in the city and is suffering from stress and anxiety, I ask how much of their time they spend in nature – in pure, uninterrupted and fully surrounded by nature moments. Most of them answer, 'Well, during the holidays I go to the sea, or the mountains in winter.' That is only two to three weeks out of an entire year. That's right! If you are only taking time to be really immersed in nature only fourteen days a year, then try carving out some more time – weekly or monthly – to have that cup filled and your body and soul come back to your essence.

Some of my most peaceful moments have been in the vast wilderness, with no phone or reception, just pure connection. When spending days or weeks outdoors, camping and far away from all the 'known', I have seen how my soul, body and mind transform. Even my skin and my face start to glow and shine. A natural rewiring of all your cells happens when you let yourself be immersed in pure nature.

CREATE YOUR NATURAL TOOLS:
CONNECTION WITH NATURE

It's time to set your own intention and plan from a place of joy and connection.

What are your favourite places to be when it comes to nature?

-
-
-
-
-
-

What do you love doing outdoors? List four things:

-
-
-
-

Which NEW thing would you be willing to experience this week?

- ....
- ....

Walking in nature is one of the best things you can do for yourself and for your mental health. I would like to add here that mental health is not something just 'for some' or a stigma or burden like many of us have been told. On the contrary, mental health is something we all have to focus on, and work on making it a priority. We've heard the importance of heart health, body health and gut health. Well, mental health is included and primary. We are integrated beings – our bodies, mind and spirit are all working together as a divine creation. If we focus only on one part, or take another for granted, we are not in balance.

The speed at which things go today, the number of emails we receive, 'likes' on social media, comments and messages, advertising and invitations and things to do – the stimuli is far too much for our brain to process. Most of us experience feelings of overwhelm, anxiety, high cortisol levels, hormonal imbalance and stress disorders.

When you create habits like being outdoors daily, it becomes as important as your most important meeting. You start to choose your self-care and this moment first, by giving yourself the time to breathe, connect and be present.

When you are walking or running for example, the one thing you have to focus on is your breath. Although we are breathing all the time, constantly, the awareness with which we do it changes the whole result. This is what yoga and pranayama is about, feeling that oneness and connection, that union with the self and it all, becoming ONE.

You can become wired and one with nature too, which means you will be wired to your natural state and way of being. The more you are wired to nature, the more you will be aware and conscious of the natural cycles that happen around, and this will have a positive impact on your health and lifestyle. Nature as we know, has cycles, periods, seasons and changes all year round. Most of the animals in the wild live according to these changes and ways of nature. Whereas us, human beings, have developed artificial ways, such as our electric light that keeps us separate from these natural cycles. This has an obvious effect on our bodies and our mind, our rest, stress levels, health, mood, appetite, and the list goes on and on.

Being in nature is so powerful and it is ultimately the place where we all come from. Where we are living now, whether we are in cities, suburbs, islands or mountains – when we go against natural cycles, we become disorganised and once again disconnected.

I can say this in first person, as I lived for many years in one of those cities that never sleeps – and therefore I didn't sleep either! My sleep pattern was irregular, I had insomnia, I would wake up in the morning feeling tired and some weeks all I wanted to do (although I couldn't voice it or do it) was to stay in bed and catch up on sleep. I would go to bed past midnight and many times had to wake up very early for work. I would start my day in front of the computer in my living room, sometimes not even going outside for a breath and having the sunlight shining in my eyes – telling my body it was actually daylight outside. Late nights did not always include books, sometimes I would get hold of a new series or movie that would keep me awake an extra two hours. And that meant less time sleeping when the sun was down, when nature was taking its time to rest before the next day arrived.

So simple, so intuitive, so natural – yet so complicated for many of us.

Most of us are sleep deprived, meaning we are not giving our bodies the minimum necessary amount of rest to restore and function. When this happens once, we might find it hard to keep up with work and our daily goals. We might feel extra hungry that day or tired, foggy in our brain and not quite able to focus. However, when it becomes a habit, and we repeat it for several years, the consequences go beyond the imaginary. Overweight and not being able to lose weight, hormone imbalance, loss or sudden rise in appetite, anxiety, compulsive thinking and more.

Last week I was talking with some fellow coaches and friends about a pivot point in my life, and the one thing that came up was precisely this point. When I left Buenos Aires to begin the journey towards following my heart, one of the main things that came to my consciousness was that I was extremely - and had been for many years - TIRED!

One of the most challenging parts of living in ashrams was waking up with the bells and dongs at 5 am. As a teacher there told me, a part of my brain - that was being challenged and rewired - just wanted to take me into shutdown mode while my spirit and consciousness were awakening. Another part was an exhausted body and mind that had been carrying the weight of not resting properly for years!

I stayed and lived for several months in temples, surrounded by pure nature. Every day, I would feel how a part of my being was able to relax and surrender more and more into deep, deep rest. I could see and understand for the first time the limiting belief by which I had lived for so long - 'Sleeping and resting means being lazy and not doing enough.'

Understanding how unnatural and awkward this belief was, was a great 'AHA' moment. I had judged, probably since I was a little girl, my need to sleep and rest, for not coping with everything that was being asked. I had to make excuses to my mum and at school when all I needed was a break and a good sleep in. I had grown into following a pattern that was a) not natural, b) not even aligned with my true beliefs, and c) not healthy at all.

I found that I needed to heal this long period of time and strong belief that seemed so rooted in my being. The medicine was to allow for silence and deep listening of my true self. To give myself the chance to realise that sometimes we follow unnatural and unhealthy patterns and habits. It might take time to accept this and discover an alternative, and heal the belief and consequence that it had ... and ... that is ok too.

It took me years to heal from this exhausted state. Years of following my heart and body when it asked me to rest. Working less or even not working if I needed to recover. Praying and meditating and going back to sleep. Living a very calm and quiet, slow-paced life, to get to feel the difference of being on the other side. It was different to constantly being in a rush and judging things like sleep as not productive or good enough.

I would often joke with my mum that although I looked like I was in my twenties my body was actually in its eighties. Whenever we were at the gym or after a hike, I would crunch like an old lady and tell her this. As funny as we found it at the time, it was a bit of a concern. How could I be so healthy in so many ways, train, eat well and yet be tired or feel so old, sluggish and heavy all the time?

If you've been or are going through the same thing, I want to tell you – I do not feel like this anymore. It is possible to regain your health and vitality. All you need to do is give yourself at least half a chance!

Psssst! Have you heard about forest bathing?

'... We suffer from nature deficit disorder, but studies have shown ... what the Japanese call shinrin-yoku, or forest bathing, can promote health and happiness.'

- Dr Qing Li / Forest Bathing

This ancient practice of spending mindful time around trees was not one I was aware of, when I moved to live by the bush in one of New Zealand's Dark Sky Sanctuaries, Rakiura/ Stewart Island. Instantly, however, my body would take me out on long walks where I would connect and bathe myself in the forest. This body, that was still healing and finding its way towards balance and restoration, would come out of the bush feeling rejuvenated. Being back home, in nature, immersed and being one with all. Taking small and conscious steps through the bush, not having a plan or anywhere to go, no precise destination, but just letting myself be there, abundantly present and wild and natural. It was a habit that started out of following my heart and intuition and is now one I recommend and repeat daily.

Living in an isolated and small community has its challenges, especially when one is used to a big city lifestyle. However, I soon started to see how things, such as my sleep, turned and changed completely by living on 'island time'. Since living by the bush, I have found that sleeping profoundly and deeply is something that I can and love to do. And most importantly, sleeping means I wake up fully rested.

There are various sleep doctors and professionals out there that can guide you even deeper and with more tools in this realm. If this is something you struggle with, explore. Ask for help, open up to new possibilities of living a life where you are rested and get to repair, where you can slow down and let everything go and regenerate and digest during your sleep. You can change and so can your sleep patterns – and they can become even better from where you are now, in this instant and what your body needs in this moment.

CREATE TIME FOR YOURSELF: CONNECTION WITH THE SELF

Make time for yourself, to make the REAL changes you want to in your life.

- **Sol Pineda**

I had another deep realisation that I would like to share with you:

In order to change your life

Where you are at now,

You must give yourself time.

Allow for time to just be,

Without doing or working.

And make this time yours

As much as you need.

What does this mean, Sol? It means you must clear space – in your day, in your calendar and busy life – to stop, and give love, care and attention to yourself.

In my busy city life, at the end of the week I would often stop to visit my grandparents. And just after entering the door I would say, 'I don't have much time. I'm rushing today so I'll be here for just a while.' I could feel the sadness and disappointment in their faces just as I finished these words – even as they started coming out of my mouth. And yet, I would go back to this excuse and survival mode type of communication repeatedly.

Just before deciding it was time to change this hectic life, I realised how often I had said this, to family, my friends, and people I loved. It was an excuse for being half present and thinking about the next moment, meeting, or event before the present moment was even over. This realisation was a before and after. I felt ashamed, embarrassed with myself at realising this excuse – and the various ways and tones in which I had used it with so many of my loved ones – just ignoring their disappointment and moving on to explain my excuse even further.

A dear friend called me and wanted to catch up. I had used this excuse with her many times in the past and she had expressed her discomfort. The moment I was about to open my mouth, I realised that this belief and mindset of not having 'enough time' was done and dusted. I was ready to replace it and work on new ways.

She asked if I would go to her place, all the way to the opposite side of the city (probably more than 1.5 hours driving in traffic). I took a deep breath in and said, 'Yes of course, I'll be there in the afternoon and stay for dinner and maybe even all night.' It was not a huge thing, and it felt so big. I felt the joy and love that came from her next words, feeling appreciated and enough with my response. I celebrated that moment. She may still not know till today, that just with that little act, and showing up to her in that way, I grew so much and shifted from a scarcity mentality to one of abundance and love.

Not having time for others translates as also not having time for yourself. I am sorry if this hurts, but this is just an excuse that we make up, not to go deep into ourselves and explore what we really need. It is an excuse not to become responsible, to honour our beings, our health and to not deal with true commitment. As my incredible lawyer and friend told me once, 'People who are constantly saying they are busy are choosing that mindset. Their busy days may be less busy than yours or mine, it's just something that they say to justify being and living in a rush mode.' And having been there, done that, I completely agree with her.

If you don't 'find' time for yourself, to deeply connect and listen to your heart, to walk, to be out in nature, care and love your body and presence, cook and eat a meal, it's simply because you're not prioritising this. The outside world, whatever that is, with the list of excuses that you may have, is reinforcing a belief that is not serving or allowing you to reflect, choose again and change. Things don't just happen; we make them happen.

How many times do we find ourselves or see people around us eating in a rush? People eat while watching TV, or talking on the phone, answering emails ... This 'habit' that may sound so simple and non-harmful, is a way of telling yourself and your body, 'Sorry mate, got no real time to nurture you – so we will just cope with what we can, and I will swallow this sandwich as I get to my next task.' Guess what?! That message is NOT what your body and digestive system would like to hear from you. Our bodies can either stress or digest. So, if you're running late to the next meeting, reading a business email that may trigger some responses in your brain, trying to supervise your kids, distracted eating will have its consequences. It can affect your digestive tract and the energy that these foods will give to your body ... There's not much nurturing in rushing around and having no time, right?

If reading this brings you emotions of discomfort or anger, just breathe in deeply and exhale – and as you do, tell yourself: 'I have all the time in the universe. I have abundant time and I choose myself first.'

Just by giving yourself half an hour in the morning or afternoon, a break through the day, or replacing some of the time using various devices (phone, computer, TV, etc) for some other type of leisure, you are already rearranging and creating that space and caring within.

One of the things that made me fall in love with my partner in a profound and new intimate way, is the way he approaches and moves in and through nature. In the bush, in the mountains, the deep sea or wherever he is, he becomes one.

Listening to all that he had to share in the beginning when we would go for a walk or a swim, had my mind in full alert mode. Gently but consciously, he would talk about the trees, its exposure to the sunlight, their orientation, the way they were surrounded by other trees and their competition for survival. He would talk about the tracks from animals and deer, their size, when they had last been there according to the smell, the rubbing in the trees, the warmth of their feces – fungi and tracks around us that I didn't even know. All of this being pointed and shown to me while walking. The winds, how they shift and what that means – there was so much to know! And I wanted to know and understand it all.

I became more conscious about my steps, not tripping in the muddy bush or on huge roots. I listened to what he was telling me, almost whispering. I remained silent as well, so as not to disturb the bush, and digesting all this information. I saw how he had all this knowledge and things to tell me, but it was not his thinking mind that was telling me this. He was not thinking like I was. He was just being ...

When I released 'the need to think' and just became an observer, I began to see clearly. I felt like a part of the bush, sensing the smells and things happening around me. I started seeing prints, and my sense of smell could detect what was happening around. I could see light between the trees and the sun's exposure that he was talking about and follow them. I could just be there and almost float through each step – as I had watched him do for so long.

The moment I could stop thinking and just observe, as he said, I started being a part of this oneness and living a sensory experience – beyond what I believed or thought I knew.

If you have the chance to be in a really wild, natural place – like a national park or reserve or a protected area – practise just observing. All that is happening around your being, everything, breathing slowly and gently. When you become the observer of life – a situation or emotion – you are a part of that moment without the need to travel in time.

CREATE PRIORITIES: A TIME MANAGEMENT TOOL

I invite you to think about everything you've done today. From house chores, family, kids, breakfast, work, travelling, using your phone or computer, social media surfing, notes that you may have taken, moments of going over the same thought again and again...

Were all these activities, these moments, a priority in your life?

Suggestion: If I would tell you this moment is IT, this is THE FINAL DAY - what would you have done for yourself? Would you have been able to reschedule and choose again? Would you have chosen yourself instead of some - or all - of the activities?

CREATE PRESENCE AND AWARENESS:
CONNECTION WITH THE NOW

When we start to live moment to moment - in this instant - the anxiety of the future and everything that we have to do for it lessens. We then realise how being present, doing things with focus, ONE at a time, brings much more joy and the opportunity to manage your life and time in a whole new way.

When you care about yourself you start to become WHOLE. We tend to seek caring from outside of us (from someone else or something) more than within. Don't get me wrong, you are not alone. I have been there, done that.

If, for example, your parents were not fully present or could not care completely for you when you were young, there's a sense of incompleteness that goes on and on, playing in your mind. If you felt rejected or secluded at school by the teacher or your peers, you are probably going to try to seek an opportunity to amend that trauma or those relationships, hence wanting to be cared for by someone or everyone else. Also, souls like myself who have grown trying to please everyone, are usually more concerned on caring for others and the outside, rather than the inside and themself. For true and lasting change to occur, for us to return to being whole, complete, and loving, we don't need a magic wand or a prince or princess – not even a time machine. What we do need and can do, is to choose to become responsible for the person (that is to say the body, the mind, spirit and soul) that you are now – and start to act from what you truly want within, instead of trying to find it outside.

There's also a limiting belief that many of us have adopted that has to do with the non-acceptance of something greater than ourselves. Many of us have grown up being taught that we have to worry constantly – and we do a lot. We live a stressful and full-on life, preoccupied with things all the time, in order to become successful.

This is an absolute contradiction with the Law of Manifestation and the allowing for something greater than yourself (aka the universe, God, spirit) to do its own work of guidance as you walk your path.

I've had clients that started our program with their main concern being their stress and worry towards the future (money, work, relationships, weight). Whatever the topic is, it is ultimately the same, your mind is in the habit of wondering and keeping you 'busy' with constant worrying.

As we go into our program with tools that have proven to work (by no means all of them are mine – these are tools that are out there and available to all), with accountability, showing up to oneself and committing, 'suddenly' a sense of relief starts to happen. More joy, less worrying. Because this has been a habit many of us repeated for so many years, it tends to become part of our personality. 'Worrying is who I am, stress is who I am.' When these clients start to feel more present, lighter in their existence, a part of them, and I quote 'is worried that I am not feeling any worries.' Oh yes, I heard this so many times.

Whenever you catch yourself in one of these traps, the tool here is to just call it out. Bring it to the light, call it by its name, say it out loud!

I have had these moments myself where I asked the universe for stillness, peace and presence. And when I received it and listened, a part of me would judge it as not being productive enough. I would think, what am I doing here? Just doing nothing instead of worrying for the week or days to come ... I also judged myself and have been judged for not having a 9 to 5 job, filling in hours doing something that I don't like to do or want to do, just for the sake of following what I 'have to' or 'should' do ...

With love and respect, I think that if a belief does not resonate with you, then following it just for the sake of 'you should' gets you stuck into a life of less joy. You start living in survival mode and according to other people's validation and perception.

As a coach told me in one of those moments where you can see the shadow of shame and low self-esteem coming up, the only one who needs to validate yourself, your work, your existence and your path, is you.

And so be it. And so it is.

You are the only person that can validate yourself,

Your work, your success, your life and path.

If you are seeking stillness and silence, and you want to live through this experience of 'being' rather than 'doing', and the universe offers you the opportunity – just grab it! Enjoy it and live it moment by moment. When the voice of 'not enough' comes up, remember that the truth of what you really want to manifest comes from a place of stillness. And there is a higher reason why you are being given the opportunity to experience this stillness. Slow down and listen to your inner self.

As you bring yourself back to your own validation, remember that you are here to be, not to do constantly.

You are allowed time off, and this is ok. Make it your mantra:

I am allowed time off,

And this is ok.

It is safe and healthy to be admiring the landscape, following a guided meditation, or sitting down under a tree listening to birds and nature. All these thoughts of it not being ok are part of an old you. Be ready and open and present to live in this moment now.

This is it, friend. This is where you are NOW.

It's safe to relax, and

*it's healthy to slow down and allow your
being to simply BE.*

No need to worry

if something doesn't feed your soul, let it go.

We will go further into this topic later as we talk about judgement. For the time being, just remember that it is ok to slow down and allow things to be. And this place of stillness is where magical shifts occur. They don't usually happen when we are in fast mode or survival mode, there we are just repeating. However, when we challenge ourselves with something new, maybe something as difficult as relaxing and slowing down or doing nothing, then we are putting something completely different into the equation. We are allowing for a new stream of thinking, of thoughts and beliefs and realities to be manifested.

This can apply as much to a busy professional, business owner, mother or father or teenager. Just let go, create time for yourself, explore something new - something unknown or something that you've never tried before. Experience being in complete and total contact with yourself. Be present and aware, and let the energy and flow of what happens deliver a message, a reflection, an observation, or simply the chance to have a healthier, present, happy moment.

You can live a life with 'no worries' as the Kiwi saying goes. It is an option, and it is a choice. Worrying will not get you closer to that result or achieving this or that, being will.

CREATE YOUR SELF-LOVE FIRST AID KIT:
CONNECTION WITH SELF-LOVE

Once we are still, relaxed, in our being without doing – this is where we can create from. You can truly create and have your music shared with the world.

As I am writing this book, I am also engaged in many other activities and jobs, together with my health coaching practice. Aiming to always keep the progress going, I've caught myself going back to old habits of over doing and less being. Whenever this arises, a part of me is already ready to go into my self-love first aid kit.

My best friend is the first one to tell me ok, it's time to go off bush, back to nature, spend some time there, meditate and then come back. This is one of my main tools, where I combine walking, nature, stillness and silence, and true listening of the soul. There's no need to plan much or always have a whole week or 'the plan'. Just grab the boots, backpack and go.

It is here where I can let my mind rest. I observe and immerse myself in the wilderness. I connect with the elements, earth, air, water, fire and come back to who I truly am - beyond work, labels, agendas and phone calls. This is part of my work, part of my routine and system of support. Having friends that remind me of it, taking time off and knowing I deserve it, holding myself accountable for a needed break.

If you happen to spend too much time inside, in front of your computer, at your desk, at home - and nature inspires you and brings the peace and connection that I have been talking about - please take this as the first element to place in your self-love first aid kit.

Now tell your best friend, acupuncturist, therapist or coach about it and ask him or her to keep you accountable. Before reaching the overwhelming state where you can feel you can no longer cope, tell yourself you can and that you have a toolbox for this. You may want to use this exercise that I have shared in many workshops.

Get a lovely small box and decorate it (you may also do this as craft time with kids).

Put in the box: post it notes, reminders, signs, or elements that remind you of your self-care and self-love routines and favourite exercises. Then when you need to get your box, you can go and grab something randomly or choose what will work for you that day.

Keep the box near your bedside table or kitchen and come back to it when you need to give yourself some first aid love.

Some suggestions:

- ◊ **Drink some alkaline water**
- ◊ **Play some mantras**
- ◊ **Singing bowls**
- ◊ **Peaceful music**
- ◊ **Going to the sea**
- ◊ **Juicing**
- ◊ **Smoothie time**
- ◊ **Sailing**
- ◊ **Fishing**

- ◊ Gardening

- ◊ Sail

- ◊ Camping outdoors

- ◊ Run, jog or walk.

CREATE CREATIVITY: CONNECTION WITH SOURCE

Let's tap into creativity.

Creative tip: Get a white canvas.

Sometimes for clarity to happen, we need to prepare a creative space. This starts with allowing yourself time and being patient, as you listen to the deep voice coming from your heart.

You may also want to clear some space physically, and make it look and vibe as you want. Whatever will support your creative space. Having a moment of creativity is giving yourself a moment to connect with the essence and source of all inspiration – pure love and presence.

Let's say you want to paint. You will need some utensils to create your painting, a white canvas, and an inspiring space. Something that nurtures and supports your soul. For me, a creative space needs to feel like my sanctuary. Candles, essences, palo santo, sage and nice colours.

Then we will move into creating a routine. Let's explore the creative way you'd like to shine your love and light with others, and how will you make space both mentally and physically for this to happen.

EXERCISE:

I would love for my creative soul to express itself by/through:

Example: I would love for my creative soul to express itself through the wonders of writing and dancing.

....
....
....
....

How will I create space for this activity in my life?

Example: By writing in my calendar a weekly appointment with myself where I just play ON in my playlist and start dancing. Then when I finish, I journal.

....
....
....
....

What will this space look like physically?

Example: I would have all the furniture moved (if I need or require to) to create some space and have a backup plan to dance in the garden. I will have my favourite dress ready, plus a playlist just for this commitment.

....
....
....

Now that you are ready to explore your creativity, I invite you to think outside the box, outside this book, and go do it! Commit and show up to your connection to source and presence ... You will find, like most artists and creatives, that from this space everything is possible. Energy flows and the mind can rest. The only thing you really need is to be fully present with yourself and what you've committed to.

This, my friend, it is the creative source of consciousness expressing its love and joy though you. However you are bringing it out from the depth of your being, it is ready and mature and wanting to come out. Let it be, just let whatever needs to come out and be expressed just be.

Chapter 8

BUILD A ROUTINE

In order to build a routine, the first thing is to have the courage and love to allow for changes to happen ...

When we can own that our excuses are no longer our friends, that procrastination is not who we are and that change can and is always happening, we can live the life we want and start creating and guiding the path towards our dreams. When you take this first step, you become ready to create space, prioritise and start practising, in order to build a routine.

In the previous chapter we talked about creating space for ourselves. This brings me to our next and correlated topic: prioritising.

YOU ARE YOUR PRIORITY.

Even when your kids, family, spouse, employees and clients may need you, you need to truly believe that you are your

priority. Prioritise yourself in order to give your best and show up for the life you want to live – a healthy life that allows you to be in the present moment, less stressed and less anxious, calmer and more focused. Prioritise your health, your habits, your physical practice, your food, your hydration, your self-care routine and your self-love supply.

Ask yourself again ...

What would you do if you had all the time in the world?

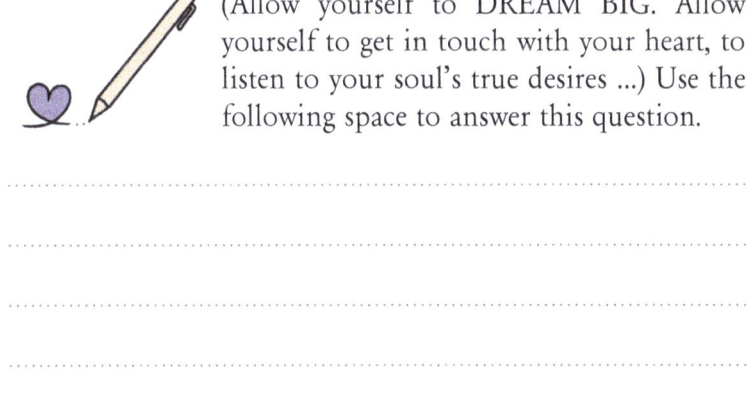

(Allow yourself to DREAM BIG. Allow yourself to get in touch with your heart, to listen to your soul's true desires ...) Use the following space to answer this question.

....

....

....

....

....

What is it that you'd love to do for yourself, practise daily and make a routine of?

....

....

....

....

What do you really want to achieve in this lifetime?

....

....

....

....

Write down all the things you want to achieve by:

The end of tomorrow:

....

....

The end of the week:

....

....

The end of the month:

....

....

The end of next year:

....

....

After moving in with my adventurous partner, having the house of our dreams in the bush, spending and creating amazing memories with our family, attending jobs with full presence, building a business, attending workshops around the country, writing a book, and having clients who also have busy and overwhelming lives, I've come to understand the importance of time management.

The thing is, time is relative, right? Some people may feel they have a lot of time, others feel they don't have enough. Sometimes time goes by slowly, and other times it can go fast, so fast you don't even realise. Whether this happens for internal or external reasons, planets aligning or moon phases, I still don't know the answer. I believe it is a combination of everything, of ALL – as we are a part of the whole. And therefore, everything that is occurring on another level, to what we know or understand, is also having an effect over us that sometimes we might not be fully aware of but can still feel.

During coaching practice I have learnt how to declare smart goals. This has helped me come back to focus and planning after taking a couple of years of doing the opposite, not doing and planning and just being.

Using goals to prioritise your activities can be a great source of focus for the mind, motivation and inspiration. Plus, it helps create order and clarity. In order to avoid those long to-do lists that only take up space in your brain – I prefer to start my day or week with no more than three main goals.

If you can commit and focus on those three goals for the day, then end up doing three more other things, great! It's a super energetic productive day. If however, you're feeling low on energy or ready to just look forward to those three goals (which may include drinking enough water, paying bills, going for a walk or catching up with a friend) then that's awesome too.

This was my way to stop making never-ending lists that would keep me overthinking and unfocused and bring up anxiety and discomfort. When you can focus on one thing at a time, start, finish it and continue to the next one – instead of trying to multi-task or get repeatedly interrupted – you are most likely to be in a clear space, able to create and achieve what you want.

The next step is to list the weekly tasks that support those goals.

EXAMPLE:

Goal 1:

....

Tasks or action steps that support this goal:

◊

◊

◊

Goal 2:

....

Tasks or action steps that support this goal:

◊

◊

◊

Goal 3:

....

Tasks or action steps that support this goal:

◊

◊

◊

One key tip is to put things in your calendar – either your phone calendar, Google calendar, agenda or reminders. Once it's placed in your calendar you are more likely to commit to these tasks and complete them. So, use your calendar as your ally and have a due date for your activities and goals. If you can set up a starting and finishing time, even better!

Eliminate multi-tasking.

Instead, create a routine.

- Sol Pineda

What happens when multi-tasking is what we believe to be true? We were either told so, because we grew up with that model, or turned to believe that this is the way to survive. Multi-tasking means that no one task has your full attention. In other words, you are lacking focus. This lack of focus, followed by repetition and 'praising' multi-tasking as something associated with success, may lead you to make repetitive mistakes, and not complete tasks. The end product can turn out less effective or accurate than what you intended or desired.

As a dear friend and coach told me:

YOU CAN DO ANYTHING – BUT YOU CAN'T DO EVERYTHING.

At least, not at the same time. Not all together, all at once. That is the equation and translation of chaos. Training your brain to focus may sound challenging – and it is the way to be fully present in what you are doing, in each moment, each task with each soul in front of you.

When you start to create small goals for each day, think of some associated conscious action steps you can take, to help make them happen. Give each of them a solo focused space in your calendar. Then you can start working on repeating it and creating a habit of what is going well and serving you now, to be present in this moment.

We are so wonderfully weird beyond what we know. When you start taking these steps into being more aware, organised and building a routine that supports you, the intuitive part of yourself will start to love these new habits, and let go of those that don't serve you anymore.

It is proven that our minds learn by repetition. So, if we schedule the same activity every day at the same time and eliminate all distractions or excuses, we are likely to create a new pattern or habit.

In his book *Breaking the Habit of Being Yourself*, Dr Joe Dispenza talks about the unconscious thoughts, emotions and behaviours that are automatically repeated that take us to a predictable future. Repeating our stories and patterns and behaviours over and over again.

> *'If you become aware of your automatic habits,*
> *and you are conscious of your unconscious*
> *behaviors so you cannot go unconscious again, then*
> *you are changing.'*
>
> **- Dr Joe Dispenza**

It's about becoming aware. It is about being able to recognise in that moment that what you are choosing is something you've been repeating.

It is either something you learn or develop, and has been part of your routine. After years and years pass, it transforms into your personality, and it's now your present moment.

Changing your habits is as easy as being aware, honest and bringing them back to the light. Back to love – and allow new thoughts of how you truly want to feel and be enter you.

A big part of a health coach's job is to help you change or release old, unnecessary habits. Personally, when I walk my talk and come back home to this realisation, every year, every season there is a new part of myself, of the self, ready to come to the surface. By allowing this process to happen with awareness and observation, I can choose to change.

Once I see it, I can choose. Once you see it, you can choose. You can choose to either repeat that thought, pattern, or habit, or to choose again. I constantly use a method (and suggest it to all my clients) that I've learnt from Gabby Bernstein in her *Super Attractor* book, called the 'Choose Again Method'. It is about being able to identify the thought or pattern or habit and asking yourself where these thoughts come from. Is it from a place of love? Or does it come from a place of fear? And then choosing again.

It is about asking for forgiveness and guidance, liberating yourself from what does not serve you anymore. Knowing that you can keep on choosing differently, something new, something that works better for you, something healthier and from a place of love. Choosing from where you truly want to feel and be.

By repeating new thoughts, the mind starts to re-learn. We can create new habits, emotions and ultimately even change our personality. This is not a superpower for just a few, this is something that you can start practising and trying for yourself today. You can start to get clear on what you want now, on how you want to feel (instead of what you don't want anymore). You can bring that feeling, all the visuals and emotions associated with this new thought, dream or goals, and feel it now.

I AM A DIAMOND

BE THE PRESENT MOMENT OF WHAT YOU WANT TO BECOME.

Just like if you had a magic wand or a genie ready to make it happen in this instant, as you think and visualise your dreams and place them on your mind, you can consider them done. Easy!

For years, instead of seeing myself as the healthy, strong, radiant and empowered woman that I felt deep within I was – I would only repeat to myself that which I didn't want anymore. How I didn't want to look this way and have these curves, or my body to be a certain shape, or food to be such a big deal both emotionally and physically.

Until I realised that all I was doing was continuing that cycle secretly from the outside world, feeling ashamed and guilty – nothing major happened or changed.

There were several moments, maybe days, where I was kind of getting close to what I wanted, and then – then all those fears of how I didn't want to feel came back. And there I was again – stuck in an unconscious repetitive cycle.

'You are not stuck where you are, unless you decide to be.'

-Dr Wayne Dyer

This also applies to how you want to feel and live life. Let's go back to the example of living life always in a rush and trying to do it all while procrastinating some of your main needs. What happens when you go out on holidays, and you get to experience something completely different? You start to feel calm, present. Your body is now relaxed, and you can allow time to slow down and observe. Why not choose to come back and apply this feeling to your daily life?

As hard as this may sound sometimes, it all comes back to YOU becoming responsible, aware and owning what the moment is trying to show you. What life and spirit are ready for you to change, what new adventures are waiting if you dare decide to come out of stagnation. And then, everything is possible. You just have to add the love ingredient, the most important one in any recipe, and you will create change, something new, something magical.

EXERCISE: ADD THE LOVE

Let's say your body image is not something you love. That there is something or all of it that feels not enough.

- ◊ **Add the love to it: I love my body and I feel enough.**

- ◊ **Visualise, create another vision board or a mental picture of this body being strong, fit, loving, beautiful and most of all – enough. Envision your Ideal Body Self and surround it with love and trust.**

Let's say your self-care routine feels the opposite of a loving one and you need to bring back the love.

- ◊ **Add the love to it: I love myself and I am my priority.**

- ◊ **Visualise, create another vision board or a mental picture where you are your priority. Think about all the opportunities where you can and you will prioritise yourself. For example, visualise yourself waking up early**

in the morning before everyone else to do your yoga stretch routine. Or maybe, envision yourself cutting your day at midday, going for a refreshing walk or run to the park.

If you are feeling like the story of where you are in life, in terms of your relationships or achievements, your career and goals is different to what you once dreamt of, then start telling that story differently by making your own mantra.

Example: I love and appreciate all that I've done so far and where I am NOW.

CREATE YOUR OWN MANTRA:

◊

◊

◊

◊

If your story around money and finances has been around scarcity, un-fulfilment or fear, then add the love.

Example: I love money. I love being able to pay for my bills. I love investing in myself and those I love. I love using the money I generate for what I want. I love having a savings account and taking part of my salary to develop a saving system and routine.

Start setting your intentions today. Honesty and clarity are your powers, and you don't need to think, try or aim at being perfect. Just one baby step a day, one sentence, one word that you are telling yourself, adding to your life. That one thing may be the gateway to letting in what comes next...

Becoming the creator

of your own life,

is your choice.

- Sol Pineda Wellness

Chapter 9

CHOOSE THE NARRATOR OF YOUR STORY

All through our journey we are mainly doing and seeking for one thing – CONNECTION.

When you sell food at a store, prepare coffee, offer a service, build houses, work at a school or for the government, meditate and do yoga – all we are doing is working for and with each other, connecting.

For some reason we have accepted this 'social contract' that we need to work in order to live, as an alternative to hunting and gathering and living as our ancestors used to.

While a side of this may be evolution and the way things are meant to be, everything, absolutely everything still starts with you. And as my mum once told me during one of those dark nights of suffering and crying, it will also end up with just yourself, this is how we came into life and it's the same way we leave. It's always been you, it will always be you. The whole journey, you are the one making all those decisions, turning those corners, engaging with those souls and developing relationships, habits, your environment, your lifestyle.

Once you go through the deep experience of listening, and you can allow for something else – beyond what you have been repeating to yourself, attaching to and ultimately making your truth – you are ready and can start to re-create your own life and be the narrator in it.

I'd like to add here that listening may not only be with and through others. Although you can listen to friends, family, enlightened wisdom and speakers, podcasts and meditations, there's another way, if not the deepest way to listen. It comes from listening to the divine, God, to nature, to what this instant and your heart tells you, the birds or just a moment of stillness and silence within.

This again may or may not require practice. It is an innate power that we all have and sometimes use without even being aware.

You can ask and connect with a higher power beyond the thinking mind. Profoundly surrendering all outcomes or expectations and just asking God, the divine, angels or souls around to direct you in the way of service and love. You don't need to be religious to have a conversation and connection with God and the divine. It has always been there for you and around you - on those dark nights of the soul when something miraculously happens, when you are admiring nature, a sunrise or a sunset, God is always there.

Not long ago I started recognising what I have read in Dr Wayne Dyer's books and heard in many speeches, that had always been here, but I didn't understand or see yet. He mentions these orbs of light that have filled his rooms, conferences and pictures, a divine presence captured by the camera.

For many years my best friend and I have seen them. We've joked about 'the light always entering' the scene, coincidences with a part of my name and the constant presence of the sun around in those pictures.

Recently, one of those beautiful afternoons, I was going to give a yoga class. As I came out of our house, this stunning sunset became the One Moment, that oneness all in one. After a couple of breaths, feeling gratitude and connection, I took this lovely picture of the moment. Once again the orb was there to illuminate and remind us to connect with God and the divine.

Some may think it's a camera defect or explain that it has to do with the light. This is where your listening and connection, your approach and reception to God is and will always be your own. If you believe in omens and they keep on appearing, in signs or divine coincidence, it's wise and inclusive to say and appreciate that this is your way to connect with the divine, with no judgement and pure trust.

And then, once you experience this moment, this One Moment, be ready to let it go. For it is just that moment, and it's enough, full and loving and the next one will come.

Stay receptive

Stay open in heart and mind

Stay innocent

Stay connected

Stay breathing

Stay in the moment

And then …

Be open and receptive to receive more of these messages when you ask for them. There is something higher than us protecting and guiding us. You are not alone, the whole is supporting the I. The more we work on the 'I/ self' experience the clearer we get to see and experience with the whole.

Even in the middle of the storm or an unpleasant part of the story, if we can think of ourselves as the narrators, then when we are ready, we can create a blank page to start again.

Starting again involves great courage. Starting again also gives you two options, to re-write what you've already written, (aka to repeat) or to write a whole new story. When you realise that you can write your story, then the voice and the tone will depend absolutely on you. How you want to feel, manifest and create in this moment, will have to do with what you are now telling yourself.

I'd like to think there are several 'ingredients' that you can never have too much of in your 'mind pantry'. Those are:

GRATITUDE. COMPASSION. KINDNESS.

Plus:

Knowing what you deserve,

That you are enough,

And that you have the power to change.

- Sol Pineda Wellness

Dr Joe Dispenza refers to this as accessing the heart's intelligence. I had never heard of this before and yet even as a young girl, I had been accessing this intelligence and coherence. You have as well.

I had heard about the different types of intelligence – social intelligence, emotional intelligence – and no one had explained to me that this applied to our hearts as well. And yet, as it may have happened to you, it was innate wisdom. Even as a little child without knowing it, I could access what my heart was saying just by pure intuition.

'... The heart is not simply a muscle or a physical pump that moves blood throughout our body, but an organ capable of influencing and directing one's emotions, morality and decision making.'

- **Dr Joe Dispenza**

Back in my school days I remember that instead of showing up with love and light, sometimes I would not be fair or judge a friend, maybe even make someone feel uncomfortable (out of my own insecurities). Whenever that happened, something inside of me would talk loud, tell me, 'Hey Sol, do you think this is the way? Do you feel at peace with this? Isn't it time to own your truth? You know this is not coherent with who you are.'

I would listen, and yet I was scared. Many times I didn't believe the voice or tried to ignore it. It would be louder, it wouldn't stop. I would go to sleep still thinking about that one instant that was not the way ...

Now I understand, it was not the way my heart knew and was directing me. I was tapping into my heart coherence at some level, but felt weak, too insecure and ashamed to follow it.

I remember back in my early teens, a beautiful soul and friend was being heavily bullied by the 'cool' group of girls in our class. I had been there before and had felt that separation, shame and fear of being alone many times but now had gotten to a more neutral position where I was not in with the cool ones but not completely out. Conveniently, I didn't voice or say anything in favour of this friend. Still, that heart coherence was coming in so loud, that I decided to go and talk to my friend's mum about this injustice and shame that I felt for not standing up for her.

Understandably enough, her mum got upset at the situation and told me that I should have done something about it and that it was not ok for me to stand in a neutral position. These words, her gestures, everything about this conversation – even the rhythm at which my heart was pumping as I talked with her – stayed with me for days on repeat mode.

As the week approached its end, I felt I had to go and talk with the headmistress about it all. I told her what happened, what I had done, how my friend's feelings were hurt, and what her mum said. Which, as much as I agreed, it was both too late and something I was not sure I could do.

She told me to just follow my heart. To find the time and when I was ready, whatever I needed to say with love would come up. And so I did. I went deep within and first forgave myself. I made space to listen to my heart, which kept on saying you are brave, you are kind, that which you are feeling and want to express so much comes from a place of love.

When the universe or the moment repeated itself in its own way, I was ready to speak from my heart. Instead of defending this other friend or saying she was not 'all that' (bullying words regarding her size, shape, curves) I just reminded the others of the wonderful, generous girl that she was. And that her love was as much as ours.

I didn't get any response – silence sometimes does speak. And after that, there was no more bullying. It had nothing to do with my voice or persona, it had to do with all of our hearts' coherence showing up.

On a side note, I will never forget that headmaster, that beautiful, empowered woman who saw a vulnerable girl and just told her to follow her heart. She gave me back not my voice, but the power to connect with my heart. Along the way, along the journey, many of these agents of love or angels come along – they probably are there for you as well – just as a reminder or a strong holding arm when we need to be brave and follow who we really are.

My father showed up as this agent of love many times. One of the most relevant moments happened when we were having some drinks in Canada by the Pacific Ocean coast and I told him I had fallen in love with a man that lived on the other side of the world, the furthermost southern point on the map. We didn't know each other quite well; we had been friends for some time and my heart felt so much love. There was something beyond what I could explain with words that happened between us. I remember my father's deep blue eyes looking at me and saying, 'You have always followed your heart, it's time to do it again.'

When we access our heart coherence, we can change a whole situation. From lowering stress and cortisol levels, to making our emotions shift and ultimately rewiring our brains as well. We can also understand ourselves and others more deeply. And we can create a bond of compassion, love, empathy and forgiveness. Accessing this heart coherence can be as easy as listening to your heart when something doesn't feel aligned with love. When your words or actions keep resonating. Or going within with a kind of discomfort. Or you think how you could have acted or done that differently (with a friend, family member, stranger). Then you have the chance to access and make the intelligence in your heart prevail.

For me, repeating words of compassion, love, forgiveness, wholeness, gratitude, health and joy, has been a way to repeat, re-wire and create a direct channel with my heart's coherence. Neuroscience now backs what I instinctively did as a little girl, just by trusting a heart full of love.

> *'It doesn't take much time to get your heart centred.*
> *Simply find a quiet moment in your day and find*
> *stillness in your body and mind by paying attention*
> *to your breath ...'*

- Dr Joe Dispenza

Our brain learns new things by repetition. If you ever have a chance to do a course with Marisa Peer (Rapid Transformational Therapy trainer, renowned speaker and best-selling author), you will learn that every thought, word and image that you put into your brain or say, has a profound power and result.

> *'Your mind doesn't care if what you tell it is good*
> *or bad, true or false healthy or unhealthy, right or*
> *wrong, it accepts and acts on your words regardless.'*

- Marisa Peer

Which means that every single word and thought that you are telling your mind, may it be joking, out of fear, not even being sure about what you are saying, or an actual truth - your mind will take it.

WORDS ARE VERY POWERFUL. YOUR MIND IS LISTENING.

So, what do you want to say? Do you want to talk about how you are not successful or loving enough, how stressed and overwhelmed you feel? How bad or down or anxious you are lately, how you have failed?

Or, do you want to make sure that you are telling your mind positive things? Tell your mind what you truly want and wish, your desires and visualisations, the emotions in which you want to vibrate, how your heart feels and wants to feel, how coherent you want to be in your mind, body and heart.

Again, this is your choice, and in order to come out of a cycle, a step into the unknown must be made. Getting out of a vicious cycle means a leap into the unknown, out of your comfort zone - creating something new. And you can absolutely do it. You are brave, enough, coherent, self-compassionate and loving.

How about telling your mind:

- ◊ **I am enough**

- ◊ **I feel grateful for today**

- ◊ **I am lovable and full of love**

- ◊ **I am growing and progressing on my path**

- ◊ **I am peaceful**

- ◊ **I am calm**

- ◊ **I have amazing coping skills**

- ◊ **Success is being with myself now, whatever I am doing and however I am doing it, being ok with it and observing.**

Dr Lissa Rankin, New York Times bestselling author of *Mind Over Medicine* and *The Fear Cure*, says that changing your thoughts can actually change how your brain communicates with the rest of your body. Going back to coherence, changing your thoughts into loving, accepting, respectful, grateful, compassionate and kind thoughts will get the brain, heart, and the rest of the body to act, move, believe and create accordingly.

Marisa Peer talks about two main things that can easily change your perception. One is the pictures that you make in your head, and the other is the words that you say to yourself – that voice that is not always coming from a place of kindness and love. This is quite aligned with a common exercise known as visualising, which we will explore together. Making a routine out of being conscious about words, images and using our imagination in our favour, can be a way to re-train ourselves and our minds.

I want to share a story here. My dear partner, the one I was talking about before, is a commercial diver, a very capable and extremely qualified diver of deep oceans. He can go down into the water and build or re-construct things if needed, repair what has been damaged. He can have a whole team under his supervision and not feel fear or uncertainty for a single moment while doing it, because he knows and trusts what he is doing. I, on the other hand, find it a great challenge to go under water, especially where we live, where great white sharks and other amazing creatures are always around.

At the beginning of our relationship, every time he would go out on a mission or jump into the water with his tanks, the pictures that appeared in my head came from a place of fear. It was absolute terror and fear, the opposite of love and trust. I remember one particular day when he told me to stay on a "Dinghy" and follow and watch for his bubbles. It's something super easy and safe, he absolutely knew what he was doing and was with a friend. However, my mind – the images and words – were so caught up on the idea of him dying that I completely lost track of his bubbles. I started sweating, palpitating and experiencing a full-on anxiety attack.

Needless to say, my experience on boats and dinghies comes all the way from being a little girl. I have completed certifications and have always been on the water one way or another. However, the fear and words and images were so horrible, that I started doing all the incorrect things and movements one can do on a small "Dinghy". As the fear kept on escalating and my hands were shaking, thinking I had no phone or reception and I had lost him, I told myself to stop. 'Just stop. Remember Sol, the images and words that you choose and that you are putting in your mind right now is what your brain is listening to.' I started instead telling myself out loud, 'He is ok, he is experienced, he knows what he is doing, plus he is having fun. I also know what I am doing, I've been on boats before, dinghies of all sorts. He will come up to surface when he is ready and wherever he is I will see him and get there to pick him up. This is the truth now.'

A smaller voice kept wanting to introduce a second opinion, however I chose to focus on the facts. He is a diver, he is experienced, he is a supervisor, this is how he has fun. I can do this, I've been here all of my life, I can handle a motor perfectly well.

These rules that I had learnt from my course with Marisa were so powerful to overcome my fear and phobia of the underwater world, which was unknown to me until then.

My ideas, the words, the images and the worst-case scenario that had been developing and forming in my mind, was the opposite of reality. Furthermore, it was the opposite of what I, or my partner, wanted it to be.

See in this case, my fear was regarding someone else, someone I profoundly love and care for. Luckily enough, he has all the power of his mind to create his thoughts and reality. I don't think, however, that energy and creating or manifesting things stops there. Meaning, that what I vibrate may have an effect on someone else, even if our ego deceives us into thinking it comes from a place of caring.

When he came out of the water I told him everything that had happened. All that I felt and experienced, the terror, the ideas that went through my mind, the anxiety and the fact that for a couple of minutes I was not in control of what I was doing. He told me it was ok, and that he could feel it all the way down there. That he looked up at the dinghy from underneath the water because something in his heart was telling him I was not right. And his response was to send me the vibration and assurance that everything was ok, that he was having fun, that he would be up at any minute and we were ok. Amazing, hey? Telepathy, heart communication and coherence, energy vibration and switching from fear to love, with metres of water and no words, just the power of mind and heart.

On another note, I'd like to add that an article in *National Geographic* about shark attacks said you are at more risk of dying under a falling vending machine than you are to be eaten by a shark. Apparently the fear of being eaten by a shark is mostly an emotional response than what reality really is.

Our emotional response vs reality can mean an abysm between what is really happening and what we think is happening. In other words, opinion vs fact. In my opinion: sharks do eat you and if you see a great white shark that's it, death awaits at that moment for sure. Fact: avoid being between a vending machine and the floor as you are more likely to 'be crashed and that's it' than by a shark attack. My next question is, what are you choosing at the moment? Are you listening to your inner voices, facts of what you've been doing and achieving, or are you listening to that voice that talks based on opinions about yourself or others?

See, it's quite a different perspective. And it will take you to live the next moment in quite a different way. This is a great opportunity to be honest with yourself and discover what the tone of the narrator inside yourself is choosing.

A couple of days ago I was practising this one exercise. As it often happens, we have the tools and then life keeps on presenting us opportunities to use them and apply them. My expectations and desire to 'make things happen now' had been telling me there's not enough time, there's so much to do Sol, what's next? And so on. The opinion kept on forming, and I could 'see/feel' it escalating inside, like a feral voice that once given a moment of attention has all it needs to keep on growing. The moment I found myself in this rather negative loop, I became aware of all these opinions that were not at all positive. I decided to put them on a two-entry chart/table, opinions vs facts. My reality was not as those opinions had been telling me. I had actually been doing a lot, and quite opposite to what the voice was suggesting, I realised it was time to slow down and observe, and let stillness and surrender guide me through the next couple of weeks.

When this voice that tells you all these opinions starts to become the protagonist of the story, I invite you to ask yourself: does the tone align with compassion, kindness, self-love and self-worth? Or is it a judgemental, hard, criticising voice that makes you feel guilty and ashamed? The answer to this will be key on how you want to experience this moment, and how you may come back to previous understanding, realignment and a new perspective.

Remember, the words, images and tone of the voice in your mind creates your reality.

ARE YOU READY to release what's not serving you anymore?

ARE YOU READY to get that white canvas and re-create your story from an abundant and fulfilling place and space?

ARE YOU READY to replace everything you've been telling yourself? That you are not enough or don't have enough, with gratitude and compassion and come back to the facts about everything that you've done and accomplished so far?

ARE YOU READY to make gratitude your prayer and feel it in every cell of your body?

If you are, then you are ready for the next chapter.

Tell yourself, shout it out loud, write it down and repeat it: I am ready, I am ready, I am ready.

I am open and I release old fears.

I am ready for the new to enter my life.

I am ready for everything I've dream of and wished for.

Write it soon and repeat it:

I am ready, I am ready, I am ready.

Chapter 10

RELEASE JUDGEMENT

I can't stress enough how transformational and life-changing Gabby Bernstein's book, *Judgement Detox*, has been for me and my journey, family and clients. Releasing judgement was something I started in my late twenties, after a decade of absolute daily judgement, shame and self-attack. I was at a good point and had made a lot of progress and understanding on areas of myself that needed light and love, when Gabby's books got into my hands, or shall I say my backpack, minutes before going on a transformational hikoi (journey) with my partner.

Judgement had been a big shadow during my adolescence, specifically with my body, and ultimately with all parts of myself. I judged my size and figure, I judged my relationships and partners, I judged myself for my choices, I judged myself in intimate moments. Even during accomplishments – I would judge if not a part, the whole of myself repeatedly. Self-judgement was like a broken record and sadly, my one and only choice at that stage in my life, or so I thought.

Most of it happened alone, in a complete solo space and inside my head. Although sometimes I would reach that point where I felt like I was sinking in deep waters and there was no coming out. I would share some, the less shameful parts, with someone close. Of course when this happens, as much as we can think we 'have it under control' or no one can notice it, this behaviour and way of treating ourselves not only affects the self, but everything around it – all other relationships and interactions, ways of seeing others, and judgement towards all.

Later down the track, in deep silence and meditation, I could bring all this up to the light with honesty and a lot of tears. I wished and asked for forgiveness, for myself and those I've judged out of my own fear and shame. I felt as if in that recognition and finally being able to see it without hiding away from it, brought me to a healing space.

However, healing sometimes takes time, stages, and repetition. Going again through those old scars with less judgement and more compassion, and a spirit and mind able to recognise and change the tone, can bring you to a completely different space.

In this particular moment, this transformation journey I was talking about, the aim was just to get off grid and back to nature – to go out into nature with my partner, and just stay there living with and from the earth for a couple of days. As I was walking and immersing myself into nature, carrying quite a heavy pack, I asked myself, 'Why would you bring books and notebooks to a hunting trip?' That's right, I am talking about a hunting trip, and I hope that you can find the compassion to understand what this first hunting trip meant for a yogi, meditator and someone that has fallen in love with a hunter and gatherer. I learnt to accept and not judge his passion and hobbies, after lots of tears, crying and doubt for a good couple of years.

I agreed to go on this hunting trip leaving all that behind. Knowing that I would walk and make peace with life and nature and the animals around, that this food would be good for us and our family, and it came from a space of love and respect with mother earth. And mainly, non-judgement towards myself or my partner.

So you probably can start to get a hint of why I was bringing this book and all these pens and notebooks with me. I knew there would be a lot of work from and with myself. A lot of acceptance to be walked and forgiveness to bring to each moment. To basically turn the page on something that had been a judgement for a long time in my life, and I was ready to release.

As a side note and for you to understand, I had been a vegetarian since my early teens. Being raised in a country and family of meat eaters, hunters and fishermen, this had not been an easy choice. The why and the how is something for another book, however around my choice and the idea of eating meat and animals, there was a lot of everything – spirituality, intuition, shame, guilt, judgement ... The list continues. As much as I tried every single type of diet and approach, until I became an IIN Health Coach, I did not understand how against myself and my body I was going in so many ways. According to many things related to my body, from my blood type to where I was born, how I live my life and train, meat could be beneficial in some ways. The one thing that I still needed to do before trying if it worked for my body, was to release judgement.

As I was walking through the bush with my backpack, step by step, moment to moment, magical things happened and manifested in nature around almost every corner. I like to think of them or see them as messages. When I'm in need of some extra assistance with a particular matter, these messages help me come back to this moment, to presence, to accepting and creating change.

After a couple of hours walking, I caught up to where my partner was waiting for me. He excitedly told me about this pond and the place he had found that I would love so much. It was late and there was no more light. Everything had happened just as it was meant to, not by us, but by something higher, as we released the need to control or judge.

The next morning, we headed to this 'magic' place. And there it was, a pond in the middle of nowhere, filled with water lilies which resembles the open lotus flower, a spiritual symbol of death and rebirth.

A moment like this had happened before in my life, in India, at my Godfather's house when I had asked for a message or sign. So this time I knew what it meant. Something inside of me was ready to die, to be completely released. The letting go stage. Then something new – a new part of myself – could come up and emerge to the surface and open, as it was touched by the light.

Every day of our ten day trip, when my partner went to hunt and gather the food, I stayed with this *Judgement Detox* book. As I grabbed it the first morning, I questioned myself again if I really needed it, if it wasn't something that belonged to the past as I actually 'don't judge so much anymore.' Every word I heard myself say, that resistance voice, was an alert and clear sign to give myself the opportunity to explore something new, to open up to releasing this judgement, big or small, that I still had to work on.

So, what came next? I can't even put it in words. I was flabbergasted, amazed, surprised beyond all that I had thought. Judgements started to come out, one by one and all of them at once. I was able to write them down, to be so honest and intimate with them, to recognise how deep, repetitive and separate from my truth they were. I also recognised my shame and guilt towards those judgements, and my judging towards judgement. This book was pure gold, and I would recommend it to everyone and anyone.

I had this vision in one of my meditations by the end of the week that I had to share this with my friends and loved ones. I was feeling lighter, happier, not ashamed. I was even seeing transformation in my body and on my skin, out of all that releasing.

I could feel the space that had been created, the opportunity to look at myself, at that inner critic, at all those voices and years and opinions and comments – this time through the eyes of love. In this trip and in this moment I could bring light to the shadow, to the areas that still needed more nurturing and love, and to let go of those that were ready to be released.

Could it be that judgement had such a profound effect on me? And others? All of us? YES. IT CAN AND IT HAS. And it can also be transformed.

During *Judgement Detox*, Gabby will guide you step by step on what and how to transform your judgement with all her love and vulnerability. I invite you to accept what judgement has caused and occupied so far, for however long you have been carrying judgements, opinions and criticism about yourself.

How much have you been limiting yourself by judgement? How much more love can you experience, if you give yourself the courageous chance to let it go?

We each have our own ways of healing. Some of us find deep understanding and lessons in books, others in messages from loved ones or strangers. Some of us need coaching and a special trusting bond to be able to release. Whatever your preferred tool is now, today, give yourself a chance to observe and listen to the judgement that has been going on inside. I listened to this for years and years. I walked through the rice fields of Ubud listening to all judgements – mine, from others, towards my childhood, my partners and my parents. This was a part of the process. It was probably the first step of the process, to be able to say and admit that yes, I judge myself, yes I've been judged and yes I have judged others. Sitting down with your pain, being able to observe the shadows and darkness within, requires a lot of courage. You have to be very courageous and take a leap of faith in order to sit down with your darkness, and many times it is easier to run away.

Once you enter this realm of self-observation and self-exploration, a whole new world awaits. Yes, you will go deep, yes, you will need support and guidance, yes, there are parts of the journey that will be hard. But on the other end, on the other side of that river through which you are swimming and those waves that you are surfing, there's a space of release. Of freedom. That is the promise of sitting down and working through your shadows.

There is freedom on the other side. There's light and there's a new beginning where all opportunities await. The moment you decide, you consciously set yourself to release judgement. May it be with yourself or old beliefs around your family and parents, about the present or things you've done in the past. You come out of the world and you can stop thinking that you are trapped and that you are a victim. Releasing judgement is like being reborn. A part of you will die - a part that no longer needs to keep having your attention and energy. A part that has been calling all this time for you to simply give it some love. To look at it again through the lens and the eyes of love.

There are situations, there's trauma that happens as we grow up, that is not easy to be released. And yet, what else do we have but to explore and give ourselves a chance?

Even with all the spiritual work and hours of meditation, being in temples and ashrams in silence, there was a lot of judgement to sit with. There were things that had been asking and ready to come up to the light, that were shouting to be let go. And until I gave them the chance, they secretly kept on limiting me and going around and around.

Starting the process of actively and consciously releasing judgement will bring you closer to freedom. Just think about this - who would you be without all the judgement and opinions (negative and limiting ones) that you've created about yourself?

....

....

....

....

Who do you really want to be?

....

....

....

....

How would you live your life at its maximum, truly, if you were not ashamed or didn't feel guilty about doing it?

....

....

....

....

....

....

There is another way. I did it, Gabby did it, many of her readers did it – and you can do it too. You can change your life. You can stop living in the 'shoulds' and conditionings. You can own your truth, your gift, what you are here for and what makes YOU unique, NOW!

One of the major doors into releasing judgement, is forgiveness.

In order to take a major step towards letting go of past and future ideas, or stories of judgement and guilt, we have to be ready to forgive – both ourselves and others.

So here I ask you, and you can be 100% honest. Are you ready to forgive?

- ◊ **Are you ready to forgive yourself for the choices you've made or didn't in the past?**

- ◊ **Are you ready to forgive yourself for those things that didn't turn out as planned?**

◊ **Are you ready to forgive your parents or other relationships that (unintentionally or out of their own suffering) may have created more suffering within you?**

◊ **Are you ready to forgive yourself for living such a busy life, disconnected from the present moment, always thinking about the last step or the next one?**

◊ **Are you ready to forgive the tone, the words, the things that you told yourself about yourself inside your head?**

What else are you ready to forgive?

In this space below you can now write a letter to yourself of what you are ready and committed to forgive, in this moment, in order to come closer to freedom.

Dear Self,

I am now ready to forgive ...

....

....

....

....

With love, abundant health

And fully present in this moment

Xxx

Signature:

Forgiveness will set you, and ALL, free. Being ready to forgive or exercising your right to be free is not always easy. It requires a lot of surrendering, plus 1/2 cup of courage, another 3/4 cup of vulnerability, 1 heaped spoon of trust and another 1 tbsp of letting go.

Going beyond this tentative recipe, forgiveness, I believe, is like nutrition, always evolving and unique to each one of us.

Is there any person or situation in your life that you are ready to forgive? Have you been holding this opinion or fact about him/her for quite a while?

I understand that when things, terrible things, things that hurt, happen (or you recall them as such), forgiveness can be difficult or even seem impossible. Whether it's your parents that hurt you or somebody in class when you were growing up, maybe a brother/sister or a friend – it is still a courageous act no matter what. There are two things that I'd like to share with you to see if this motivates or lightens up something within you, for the miracle of forgiveness to happen.

> *'All memories have an emotional component associated with them. Consequently, almost all thoughts are emotionally based, and when we recall them, we are also associating the emotions stored in our brain.'*

- Dr Joe Dispenza

When we remember something, we are not necessarily remembering the exact facts. We actually may have added to our memories with the emotion of what we felt at that moment.

So for example, let's say you remember being bullied by friends at school. You recall being in the playground with everyone around, the bully coming towards you and making you feel ashamed of yourself. When you think about it or a part of it triggers you in the present, and you live through it again, you may actually be reviving it with all the emotions that you felt at the moment. 'This person is so angry, so full of rage bullying me. He might even come and hit me. I'm scared. He is strong and I'm weak. Why would he be so mean? Everyone is here but they are not doing anything, so they are actually with him and they are also hurting me ...'

The moment I understood this truth, I could let go of a lot of the 'facts' that I had built on situations that happened in the past. It was not easy, and my mind did not agree with this statement at the beginning. But the more and more I read it and listened to it, I understood that actually yes, I had been hurt. Yes, that event may have happened, but all the factors and emotions, and colours and condiments that I was adding to them were not necessarily the reality – they were only keeping me in a wheel like a hamster, going along a story that maybe was not even that accurate or true to begin with.

Forgiveness is a courageous step into your own freedom. Forgiveness is a huge step, it's a door that may require you to revisit a space you don't want to go into. However, every time you exercise the divine right to forgive (yourself and others), you will discover that miracles will unfold from this one step.

Exercise on Forgiveness:

If you are still judging the things that you haven't done yet – are you ready to forgive and let go? To help you with this, I invite you to do a bucket list in reverse. That means listing all the things you have overcome, achieved, moments where you shined your light with the world, all the obstacles and people that you were able to forgive, and all the instants where you were present and full of love:

Example:

- ◊ **I overcame the fear of abandonment and not being enough in my relationship.**

◊ **I overcame the fear of speaking in public years ago in one of my workshops in Queenstown.**

◊ **I overcame the bitter feeling and pain that I had been holding for years with someone very close to me.**

....
....
....
....
....
....
....
....
....

If there are things or judgements/beliefs still holding you back from being your highest self, from shining your love to the world and sharing your gift – are you ready to let go?

I LET GO ...

Example: I let go of the shame and limiting belief of being an impostor and the lack of confidence in myself.

....

....

I LET GO

....

....

I LET GO

....

....

I LET GO

....

....

I am now ready to forgive:

- ◊ **My little inner child who was hurt and acted from a place of insecurity**
- ◊ **Judgements that I heard and got attached to growing up**
- ◊ **My judgements and actions towards my body.**

I feel free now:

- ◊ **I feel free now in my own body and skin.**

- ◊ **I feel free now in my relationship with my parents.**

- ◊ **I feel free now in my intimate and romantic relationship.**

Continue to practise forgiveness in your life. If you find resistance coming from your mind or ego, try using one of these mantras that can be very helpful:

- ◊ **Dear [your name] … Do you want to be right or do you want to be happy?**

- ◊ **I choose to forgive no matter what. Forgiveness is my right and will set me free. I choose forgiveness instead of …**

I always like and suggest the act of conscious free writing. It allows a place and space where we can be truly honest and fair with ourselves and the world. This last one is a point I'd like to go further into. Fair looks different or unique to each one of us. It's kind of like our taste buds – what's bitter and repels your taste buds may not be for me, and the same with fairness. Coming back to the level of fairness with yourself and your own narrator. Is your inner critic too hard, too strict? Is being like this a shield you've developed to hide and not be honest with yourself?

Could you bring that forgiveness and compassion to the present moment, to that list of all the things you've accomplished, gone through or overcome – and give yourself a hug? Can you make peace and be in love with who you are now? Tell your narrator that from now on, this is the tone that you choose. 'This is how I will talk to myself, about myself and to others!' Moment to moment!

If you are ready to change the tone of your narrator, to go from a drama and self-condemning story, to one of compassion, forgiveness and understanding – every moment that you live from now onwards will have a new colour. And this is my promise to you: you will be wearing the glasses of love and acceptance, and when you do, life, its colours, every instant, changes. You will stop going to the past so much, and become aware if you are doing so, and you will live in this present moment with presence and non-judgement.

A new narrator means that a new story is about to start. A new chapter of your life, a new beginning. It means that everything is possible and that being trapped outside of this moment is not your choice anymore. You can tell your narrator to come back to this moment, you can bring your awareness to it, to this voice, to where you are directing your life course, to where you actually want to be. And this is easy, it does not require hours of sitting in meditation or amazing practices. It can happen in this instant, as you read these words and you just bring yourself back to the now.

I am here now.

I am this instant.

And this too shall change.

This too shall pass, as everything does.

And that is ok.

Being coherent with your heart, from my understanding, is being coherent with what your heart wants now. It might be creating something, it might be moving, journaling, cooking, eating great whole foods, being with your family, talking with friends, contemplating nature or just being here, present, just breathing in and out for one instant ...

And ... if you achieve that one instant, something magical usually starts to happen. You start to be in tune with each instant. You understand without even trying or using your mind through challenges and goals, that living here and now, in this instant, is much easier than what you ever thought.

It is something for all of us. It is a gift, a discovery that you can do for and by yourself. It is the way to change your life from one of anxiety, fear and living somewhere else in your mind, to coming back and being present here and now.

Chapter 11

CELEBRATE MAGICAL MOMENTS

I talked about this book today with my best friend. I wanted to share this moment, this instant, being so present and vibrant with this work that I could breathe and exhale confidence and love, while being in presence. Because when we are here, like when we are feeling grateful or practising gratitude in our daily journal or prayer, when we are in the now, there is no doubt or worry, we just are – one.

With birds and nature, and the music of trees and wind as our background and the awareness of who we really are. Love. Being in this instant is simply about being in love with life now. It's appreciating this moment for what it is, with everything and anything that it has and that has brought you here, honouring that beautiful, sometimes uphill journey, with all its storms and its sunrises, with every choice and decision that you made on the way, and that makes you who you are.

You are already amazing, successful, abundant and in love. You made it here and you are in the now as you read these words and breathe.

So, take a deep breath in and feel the now.

NOW, WELCOME THE NOW.

As you welcome the now, your practice may take you through beautiful moments of enlightenment, of awareness of who you truly are and the world around you. Of oneness, love and being just a speck of dust. A single instant and moment in this ever-changing dynamic of life. Your ego or past beliefs may find it challenging, as they are used to acting, thinking and being in a certain way. This ego voice and other parts of your self may want to bring you back to old beliefs.

When and if that happens, you can just remind yourself that you are ready to change, that resistance is part of the journey and it's ok. You embrace it and accept it with love and compassion, with a deep breath. Remind yourself, say it out loud or within: 'I am here and now I take a deep breath and I come back to the present moment.'

When you come back to the present moment, whether it's on your first shot or after a couple times repeating this to yourself, you are clearly now living in this instant and being present in this moment. Learning, trying, progressing, coming back, releasing, letting go and becoming a whole new self. It's therefore time for one last thing, CELEBRATION!

Chapter 12

BACK HOME, BACK TO LOVE

My friend and I are both celebrating this moment – our confidence in who we are, in the fact that we want to be more present and here. We are committed to it. And slowly, with deep love and some work, we are doing it. We are actually achieving what we've always dreamed of – being in the now and living within this awareness, with less doing and more being, releasing the need to live by other people's 'rules' of what happiness is, and bringing clarity and peace to each instant.

SHANTI SHANTI SHANTI

PEACE PEACE PEACE

This is what you feel when you sit down by a lake or river, on a rock, at the wharf waiting for a boat to pick you up, or in the bush – just listening, meditating, breathing. It brings relief to your heart and mind. You can allow yourself just to BE, feeling peace and calmness and the sense of being one.

When we are present, that magical moment makes us feel connected – with everyone and everything. With friends and strangers and co-workers and people you just cross in the street. Everyone becomes your brother or sister, and you remember what you might have forgotten from rushing so much – that you are this instant. This one moment and you are here now.

Let's celebrate your creation and uniqueness.

As you read through this last step, take a moment to deeply breathe. As you exhale, feel the beautiful creation and realisation of being here.

Realising that we are each instant, is a miracle in itself. It's the journey or door towards presence and more and more joy and peace within. It's like realising that maybe all this time running towards and from something, being chased by thoughts and lack – has been just an illusion.

You've always been here and now and you can always return to this instant. When you do so, you'll find what you're really looking for – that calmness and presence, that love and connection with self.

Living in this instant, moment to moment, is a way to heal your life, and finally assume full responsibility for who you are now. This is YOUR LIFE, this moment and how you choose to live through it makes a whole difference. This is it.

Celebration letter:

Dear Self,

I am celebrating this moment ...

....

....

....

....
....
....
....
....
....
....
....
....
....
....
....
....
....
....

With love, abundant health

And fully present in this moment

Xxx

Signature:

If you've been guided to this book and this final chapter, you can rest assured that you've always been guided - by your being, by the source of love, and you will continue to be guided.

Whenever you are in doubt about this, just take a minute to look at your whole life, everything you've done so far, worked on, and experienced. Everything you've created has been a work of abundant love and manifestation. All of this shows up in the now.

Celebrating is a practice that will get you even more in touch with each instant. During my studies in economics - a science that studies human behaviour - I learnt that the mind tends to highlight the losses more than our wins. And this, as all, is just one more behaviour that we can choose to re-write and replace with a new one.

By choosing to celebrate the miracles that you create in your life, you can start celebrating every instant when you feel connected to the present moment. Every breath, every step, every word and every thought. Recognising and celebrating miracles will create a new path in your mind, your brain will now understand how to create change.

The return to love, to the present moment, is a constant practice, and you will want to have this guide, and other guides and angels to assist you to do it. Staying open and receptive is a big part of the magic that occurs. You've opened a door now, and it's about opening other doors, keeping the flow and the spirit of presence and love welcome and coming back.

You will find times where returning to love, to who you really are and being consciously present and happy in this moment, will be easy and natural. At other moments you will find it harder. Ultimately it is all the same. It's about the exercise and showing up to observe and be present without any judgement or wanting it to be different. It is about acknowledging that there's much more to what we think, feel and sense in each moment. There's a whole other spectrum and part of our self (the presence that can also be called the self or consciousness), that is present here.

And this self and consciousness can't be judged. It's not affected by what happens around it. It is always here and has always been, and will continue to be.

Consciousness is sometimes not an easy term to understand, probably because deep within there's nothing to understand. Consciousness knows, consciousness is already love and has always been, and it's about how much we return to it (or stay in it for some).

It's also not about intending or trying. My last suggestion here is not to try. Don't try anything, just let it sink in and let it be. Let your consciousness and love do its work. Come back when you feel your wandering mind is ruling the show, when you feel lost in thoughts or expectations, or when you need to focus and need a reminder of the present moment. When you start breathing and being it, just let that be and continue its flow.

Talk about it with friends and family, and even with strangers, and you will see that they all 'know', even if they don't know they know. Make this an exercise, take any of these steps or questions or discoveries you've made from this book, to share with someone else. If you feel inspired, inspire others by telling them about it. If you feel unstuck, go out and shout it all about and dance around. If you feel present, let someone know, or yourself, when this happens.

Life is a miracle in itself. Life is a wonderful vehicle to discover, explore, learn and feel and return to love. Use this life to experience and experiment with love and through love. Decide to wear the glasses of love and see life with loving colours and shapes and figures and words. Remind yourself and your mind that love is your essence. It's your truth and who you really are. Dare yourself to live a different life, one that does not need to be absent or rushing or chasing or suffering constantly. A life that can have moments of just being, of celebrating, of non-judgement and presence. Of dreaming and coming back to the now, of intention and setting yourself for love.

Love is the cure to all. Love is what we all need most. Love is what we all want. We just disguise it with different names, numbers, masks, and shiny material things.

So, are you ready to live a life filled with love?

Are you ready to wear your lens of love and start seeing all the beautiful colours, things, places and people that you are connected with and become a part of every day?

I AM.

And I am here to hold your hand. This is just the beginning. You've started to take the dust out of those old glasses that had so much judgement and fear and guilt, and you can see clearly now. The rain has gone, the storm has passed. There will be others, that's the nature of life – however your whole perception of life can change NOW. Ultimately, everything that we create and how we experience it, is about perception.

What is your perception of this moment? How can you look at this instant through the eyes of love?

I am so grateful to have walked this journey with you, as it mirrors my own readiness to change. Living a happier, healthier and more honest life takes daily work and commitment. There might be some progress and change on the outside, some things that will clearly come to your acknowledgment – others will take more time. And that is ok too, it is part of our journey here. Experiencing all the things that life has to bring ... and choosing how we want to perceive them.

The magic about perception is that it can be as positive and as accurate or realistic as you want it to be. It will probably not be the reality – for what is reality, but what we choose to believe in?

The compilation of this book has to do with changing our mindset and our perception of our own self. Why? Easy, you've heard this one before, it all starts with you. When you change your perception of the world around you, the world around you changes as well. When you dare to come out of constant repetition and the same cycle, you open the door to new opportunities and magic waiting to happen.

I live my life with gratitude every day. Whenever a setback or uncomfortable situation presents itself, I choose gratitude instead. Gratitude for the lesson, for the part of myself that is coming up to the light, for what I am ready to let go of and grow from.

As I write these last words, we are out on the boat going through the inlet and the different islands within the island, the sun is setting and all we can see is the rays of lights penetrating the different trees, rocks and illuminating a path through the water towards the horizon. I am with friends and my partner, it's four of us, all captured by the moment. There is nothing to say, silence speaks louder than the words.

We are fully present, feeling the wonder of the universe. A feeling of wholeness runs through the whole being, there's much more than what we are seeing that is present here. There so much presence. I do not need to capture this moment with my phone, upload it to social media or even share it with my loved ones. As my heart is so present, I can understand that there's a power beyond what we know, beyond what we can understand, that connects us all. That brings us all back to the now. This power I am talking about is present in this moment. And I am choosing to feel it and be here with it.

The next instant is completely different, new and unique. It is another moment, not like the one before, simply new. The invitation here is to live life through each moment, as the sunrise or as a sunset that lasts only a couple of seconds, so does everything we do, choose and think.

We can choose how to live the next one. You can choose how to live this instant.

May it be with love.

May you feel free.

May you be happy.

NOW.

You will find that all we explored in this book is about the self. Prioritising yourself, choosing how you want to live your life and talk to yourself. Visualising and creating your own reality, again and in every moment. This is the first step, starting with you, with the self.

When we create a kinder, more present self, we can become one with the whole. We start to experience and see things in a whole new way. Our next journey together will be about how we bring more love to those relationships and interactions and the world outside of you.

This has just started. A whole new reality awaits once you feel confident and complete with yourself. Remember it's about progress, not perfection. One day at a time, one instant of becoming fully present and creating the life you want.

Xo xo

Sol Pineda

ABOUT THE AUTHOR

Sol Pineda is a certified Health and Wellness Coach, Integrative Nutrition Health Coach (IIN), with a degree in Economics. She is also a Certified Yoga Teacher and Animal Flow lover who is passionate about spirituality, holistic healing, and how the brain, gut and body functions. Just like you, she is a soul with a purpose – trying to find her way back to love, peace and being in expanded and constant awareness.

Sol lives on Stewart Island, tucked away from the world at the southern end of New Zealand, with her loving partner and family. Every day she thrives doing what she loves, being a better, kinder version of herself, writing and helping others in her community.

In her pursuit towards happiness and peace, Sol has travelled the world, connecting with many people along the way. Meditation and coaching have been the pillars of her business, Sol Pineda Wellness, where she offers diverse courses and coaching programs for everyone.

Sol is a proud member of Health Coaches Australia and New Zealand Association (HCANZA). She can be reached through her website or social media.

Website: www.solpinedawellness.com

Email: hello@solpinedawellness.com

Instagram: @solpinedawellness

For more information, updates and useful links please visit:

www.youarethisinstant.com

ABOUT THE ILLUSTRATOR

Marina Remmer studied interior design and photography while working as a model. For many years this allowed her to travel, appreciating art through the world. She discovered that mandalas are great company everywhere, always making you feel better and bringing inner peace. When Marina started drawing her own mandalas, Pajarito Art was born to bring love messages from the universe.

Trusting her intuition and playing with her creativity and her inner child is how she creates and became a self-taught artist. Marina's inspirations include nature, the cosmos, eyes, women, and the magic she sees in the universe. She believes that we create our own reality, nature is our home, we are citizens of the world and love is the answer.

Pajarito Art is here to pass on these messages of light.

Instagram: @pajarito.art

Facebook: www.facebook.com/universopajarito

For more information, updates and useful links please visit:

www.youarethisinstant.com

www.ingramcontent.com/pod-product-compliance
Lightning Source LLC
Chambersburg PA
CBHW041307110526
44590CB00028B/4270